Rights and protest
Study and Revision Guide

Philip Benson

Rights and protest
Study and Revision Guide

PAPER 1

Philip Benson

Caution: several of the historical extracts and quotations in this book contain words that are vulgar and offensive.

Hachette UK's policy is to use papers that are natural, renewable and recyclable products and made from wood grown in sustainable forests. The logging and manufacturing processes are expected to conform to the environmental regulations of the country of origin.

Orders: please contact Bookpoint Ltd, 130 Park Drive, Milton Park, Abingdon, Oxon OX14 4SE. Telephone: (44) 01235 827720. Fax: (44) 01235 400401. Email education@bookpoint.co.uk Lines are open from 9 a.m. to 5 p.m., Monday to Saturday, with a 24-hour message answering service. You can also order through our website: www.hoddereducation.com

ISBN: 978 1 5104 3235 2

© Philip Benson 2018

First published 2018 by
Hodder Education,
An Hachette UK Company
Carmelite House
50 Victoria Embankment
London EC4Y 0DZ

www.hoddereducation.com

Impression number   10 9 8 7 6 5 4 3 2 1
Year   2022 2021 2020 2019 2018

Cover photo © PhotoQuest/Getty Images
Produced and typeset in Goudy and Frutiger by Gray Publishing, Tunbridge Wells
Printed in Spain

A catalogue record for this title is available from the British Library.

Contents

Case study 2: Apartheid South Africa 1948–64

How to use this book

- Welcome to the *Access to History for the IB Diploma: Rights and protest: Study and Revision Guide*. This book has been written and designed to help you develop the knowledge and skills necessary to succeed in the Paper 1 examination. The book is organized into double-page spreads.
- On the left-hand page you will find a summary of the key content you will need to learn. Words in bold in the key content are defined in the glossary and key figures list (see pages 118–21).
- On the right-hand page you will find exam-focused activities related to and testing the content on the left-hand side. These contain historical sources such as text excerpts or photos and cartoons and questions so that you can develop analytical and critical-thinking skills. Answers can be found at the back of the book.
- At the end of each chapter you will find an exam focus section. Here, you will find student answer examples with examiner comments and annotations to help students understand how to improve your grades and achieve top marks. There is also a 'mock exam' set of questions for you to try.

Together, these two strands of the book will provide you with the knowledge and skills essential for examination success.

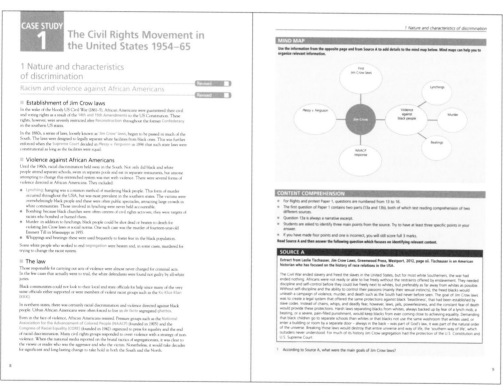

Key historical content   Exam-focused activities

At the end of the book, you will find:

- Glossary, Key figures and Timeline – key terms in the book are defined, key figures are highlighted and key dates are included in a timeline.
- Answers for the exam-focused activities are provided.

Getting to know the exam

The four questions on Paper 1 assess different skills and knowledge. You must answer all four and have one hour to do so. For Paper 1 Rights and protest, questions are numbered 13–16. The question types are as follows:

■ Question 13: direct questions

Question 13 is worth 5 marks and has two parts, both of which test your understanding of two different sources. You need to answer both parts of the question by reviewing the source material and paraphrasing information from the sources.

■ Question 14: value and limitations of a source

Question 14 is worth 4 marks and asks you to **evaluate** a source using the source's origin, purpose and the content you are presented with.

- The origin of a source is its author or creator. This might include the date, publisher and type of delivery, which could be a book, speech, propaganda poster or diary entry.
- The purpose of the source explains what the author was trying to do, such as explaining the impact of an event or conveying a certain type of information.
- The content of the source can indicate many things, such as the point of view of the author, evidence of some historical event or its interpretation or, in the case of a cartoon or other visual source, the audience that the creator wished to reach.

The values and limitations will vary according to each source. A value could be that the author of the source witnessed the event or is an acknowledged scholar. An example of a limitation could be that an author was involved in events and therefore may be less objective. You should try to explain at least two values and two limitations per source, although this may not always be possible.

■ Question 15: compare and contrast

Question 15 is worth 6 marks and asks you to **compare and contrast** two sources in terms of what information they convey to historians studying some aspect of this prescribed subject.

- Comparing means that you explain the similarities between the sources.
- Contrasting explains how they are different.
- You should aim to have about three similarities and three differences.

■ Question 16: essays integrating knowledge and sources

Question 16 is worth 9 marks and requires you to use all the sources in the examination, and to integrate them into an essay that also contains your own knowledge.

■ The appearance of the examination paper

■ Cover

The cover of the examination paper states the date of the examination and the length of time you have to complete it: one hour. Instructions are limited and simply state that you should not open it until told to do so and that all questions must be answered.

You will have five minutes reading time in addition to the one hour allotted for Paper 1. You should examine the four sources and questions during these five minutes. You are not allowed to use your pen during the reading time. However, once you are told you can begin to write, do mark up the exam paper by underlining or highlighting relevant passages.

■ Sources

Once you are allowed to open your examination paper, you can turn to Prescribed subject 4: Rights and protest. There you will see four sources, each labelled with a letter. There is no particular order to the sources, so Source M could potentially be a map, a speech, a photograph or an extract from a book. Source M is no more or less important than Source N, or Sources O or P. If you see square brackets, [ ], then this is an explanation or addition to the source by the creators of the examination and not part of the original source. Sometimes sources are shortened and you will see an ellipsis, three full stops (…), when this happens.

■ Questions

After the four sources, the four questions will appear. You need to answer all of them. It is better to answer the questions in order, as this will familiarize you with all the sources to be used in the final essay on question 16, but this is not required. Be sure to number your questions correctly. Do not use bullet points to answer questions, but instead write in full sentences when possible. Each question indicates how many marks it is worth, for example, [2].

Good luck with your studies and the exam!

The Civil Rights Movement in the United States 1954–65

1 Nature and characteristics of discrimination

Revised ☐

Racism and violence against African Americans

Revised ☐

■ Establishment of Jim Crow laws

In the wake of the bloody US Civil War (1861–5), African Americans were guaranteed their civil and voting rights as a result of the **14th and 15th Amendments** to the US Constitution. These rights, however, were severely restricted after **Reconstruction** throughout the former **Confederacy** in the southern US states.

In the 1880s, a series of laws, loosely known as **'Jim Crow' laws**, began to be passed in much of the South. The laws were designed to legally separate white facilities from black ones. This was further enforced when the **Supreme Court** decided in *Plessy v. Ferguson* in 1896 that such state laws were constitutional as long as the facilities were equal.

■ Violence against African Americans

Until the 1960s, racial discrimination held sway in the South. Not only did black and white people attend separate schools, swim in separate pools and eat in separate restaurants, but anyone attempting to change this entrenched system was met with violence. There were several forms of violence directed at African Americans. They included:

- Lynching: hanging was a common method of murdering black people. This form of murder occurred throughout the USA, but was most prevalent in the southern states. The victims were overwhelmingly black people and these were often public spectacles, attracting large crowds in white communities. Those involved in lynching were never held accountable.
- Bombing: because black churches were often centres of civil rights activism, they were targets of racists who bombed or burned them.
- Murder: in addition to lynchings, black people could be shot dead or beaten to death for violating Jim Crow laws or social norms. One such case was the murder of fourteen-year-old Emmett Till in Mississippi in 1955.
- Whippings and beatings: these were used frequently to foster fear in the black population.

Some white people who worked to end **segregation** were beaten and, in some cases, murdered for trying to change the racist system.

■ The law

Those responsible for carrying out acts of violence were almost never charged for criminal acts. In the few cases that actually went to trial, the white defendants were found not guilty by all-white juries.

Black communities could not look to their local and state officials for help since many of the very same officials either supported or were members of violent racist groups such as the **Ku Klux Klan (KKK)**.

In northern states, there was certainly racial discrimination and violence directed against black people. Urban African Americans were often forced to live in *de facto* segregated **ghettos**.

Even in the face of violence, African Americans resisted. Pressure groups such as the **National Association for the Advancement of Colored People (NAACP)** (founded in 1905) and the **Congress of Racial Equality (CORE)** (founded in 1942) organized to press for equality and the end of racial discrimination. Many civil rights groups responded to overt violence with a strategy of non-violence. When the national media reported on the brutal tactics of segregationists, it was clear to the viewer or reader who was the aggressor and who the victim. Nonetheless, it would take decades for significant and long-lasting change to take hold in both the South and the North.

MIND MAP

Use the information from the opposite page and from Source A to add details to the mind map below. Mind maps can help you to organize relevant information.

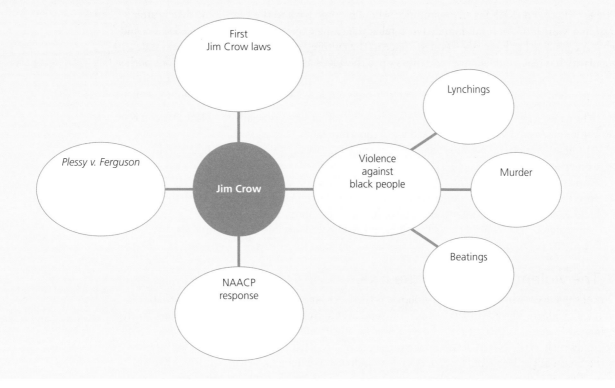

CONTENT COMPREHENSION

- For Rights and protest Paper 1, questions are numbered from 13 to 16.
- The first question of Paper 1 contains two parts (13a and 13b), both of which test your understanding of two different sources.
- Question 13a is always a narrative excerpt.
- Students are asked to identify three main points from the source. Try to have at least three specific points in your answer.
- If you have made four points and one is incorrect, you will still score full 3 marks.

Read Source A and then answer the following question which focuses on identifying relevant content.

SOURCE A

Extract from Leslie Tischauser, *Jim Crow Laws*, Greenwood Press, Westport, 2012, page xii. Tischauser is an American historian who has focused on the history of race relations in the USA.

The Civil War ended slavery and freed the slaves in the United States, but for most white Southerners, the war had ended nothing. Africans were not ready or able to live freely without the restraints offered by enslavement. They needed discipline and self-control before they could live freely next to whites, but preferably as far away from whites as possible. Without self-discipline and the ability to control their passions (mainly their sexual instincts), the freed blacks would unleash a campaign of violence, murder, and death such as the South had never before seen. The goal of Jim Crow laws was to create a legal system that offered the same protections against black 'beastliness', that had been established by slave codes. Instead of chains, whips, and deadly fear, however, laws, jails, powerlessness, and the constant fear of death would provide these protections. Harsh laws separating blacks from whites, always backed up by fear of a lynch mob, a beating, or a severe, pain-filled punishment, would keep blacks from ever coming close to achieving equality. Demanding that black children go to separate schools than whites or that blacks not use the same washroom that whites used, or enter a building or room by a separate door – always in the back – was part of God's law, it was part of the natural order of the universe. Breaking those laws would destroy that entire universe and way of life, the 'southern way of life', which outsiders never understood. For much of its history Jim Crow segregation had the protection of the U.S. Constitution and U.S. Supreme Court.

1 According to Source A, what were the main goals of Jim Crow laws?

The Ku Klux Klan

■ The beliefs of the KKK

The Ku Klux Klan (KKK) is an organization whose roots go back to the years immediately after the Civil War (1861–5). It was founded to combat the rising expectations of newly freed slaves and what it considered to be northern interference in the culture and customs of the southern states. Its popularity has risen and fallen several times since the 1860s and has appeared in all regions of the USA. After the Supreme Court's unanimous *Brown v. Board of Education of Topeka* decision in 1954, southern racists again joined this secretive organization. KKK groups shared common beliefs:

- White race supremacy: the white race is superior to all others, especially the black African one.
- White nativism: North America belongs to the white race.
- Anti-immigration: immigrants will dilute the racial purity of the nation and take jobs from white people.
- Anti-communism: communists are trying to take over the USA.
- Anti-Catholic: Catholics' loyalty is to the Pope and not the US government. Catholics are often of 'foreign' heritage. Protestantism is the only acceptable form of Christianity.
- Anti-Semitic: Jews control the global financial system and are the brains behind the Civil Rights Movement.

■ The violent activities of the KKK

One of the largest white supremacist groups was the US Klans, Knights of the Ku Klux Klan, founded by Eldon Edwards in 1953. After the Supreme Court decision, its membership grew to an estimated 12,000–15,000 by 1958. The KKK was greatly upset by the slow but steady progress made by groups such as the NAACP. Without strong action, it was felt that the segregated way of life in the South might be altered forever. A violent and vicious campaign began. In 1959, 530 overt cases of racial violence and intimidation were recorded. These included beatings, floggings, cross-burnings and bombings. Thirty black churches were fire-bombed in Mississippi alone. Among the most shocking crimes committed were:

- 30 January 1956: Montgomery home of Martin Luther King, Jr bombed.
- May–December 1961: Freedom Riders severely beaten at various locations.
- 15 September 1963: 16th Street Baptist Church in Birmingham, Alabama bombed; four young girls died.
- 21 June 1964: three young civil rights workers, Chaney, Goodman and Schwerner, were abducted and murdered by the Klan in Mississippi.
- 25 March 1965: Viola Liuzzo, a Michigan mother of five, was shot dead by the Klan in Alabama for helping the Selma marchers.

■ Federal reactions to KKK violence

In most cases, the Klan's violence achieved the opposite result of their intentions. The horrible scenes of violence that appeared in the newspapers and on the evening TV news forced a reluctant national government to take action it might otherwise not have taken. For example, the murders of Chaney, Goodman and Schwerner led the administration of President Lyndon B. Johnson to put pressure on the Federal Bureau of Investigation (FBI) to become an effective Klan-fighting force.

Furthermore, instead of frightening off the civil rights workers with violent acts, the Klan helped to create a young, courageous and resolute new generation of activists who were willing to make great sacrifices in order to confront segregation.

CONTENT COMPREHENSION

Answer the question which follows the source. Use the table to come up with at least three items in your answer.

SOURCE B

Extract from an interview with Imperial Wizard Eldon Edwards by Mike Wallace, 5 May 1957, Harry Ransom Center, University of Texas, Austin. Edwards was the leader of one of the largest Klan groups. Wallace was a well-known TV journalist.

WALLACE: … In one piece of Klan literature that you furnished us it is charged … quote … 'One drop of Negro blood in your family destroys your white blood forever'. I take it that you believe that.

EDWARDS: Well, I wouldn't, I wouldn't define it down to one drop … now. But here it stands to reason as common sense, that Mongolization means destruction … it means the destruction of the white race … it means the destruction of the Nigger race.

EDWARDS: I sure will believe in segregation for the simple reason we believe in preserving and protecting God's word. He created the white man. He intended for him to stay white. He created the nigger. He intended for him to stay black. And we believe that Mongolization destroys both races and creates a Mongol which is not a race.

WALLACE: You do believe then, a mixing of the blood of Negro and white, will lead to the downfall of the white race and of the Negro.

EDWARDS: That's right. And eventually the destruction of this country.

WALLACE: Well, I'm sure that a good many Klan members, whether in the Armed Forces during the Korean War or the Second World War, Mr. Edwards, and that some of them were wounded and needed blood transfusions. We were told last Friday by Col. Bryant Fenton, Executive Officer to the Office of the Army Surgeon-General that quote 'Blood segregation is not practiced in the Army Medical Corps.'

WALLACE: In other words, some of your Klansmen probably have Negro blood in their veins, a fair amount of it right now, as a result of transfusions that they received in the Army. By those circumstances, under those conditions, does that mean that they are not white men any longer?

EDWARDS: Well, it could show up in the offspring.

2   What, according to Source B, were the dangers in race mixing?

Danger 1	
Danger 2	
Danger 3	

Disenfranchisement

■ Reconstruction

When the North defeated the Confederacy in 1865, male former slaves were recognized as US citizens and soon gained the right to vote. For roughly a decade, during Reconstruction, hundreds of thousands of new voters freely exercised their right to elect politicians to represent them at the local, state and federal levels.

■ Restrictions on black voters

However, this situation changed after Reconstruction ended. White people began to reassert their power and created ways to disenfranchise black people. State constitutions were amended to allow this to occur and the results were significant. For example:

- In Louisiana in 1896, slightly more than 130,000 African Americans were registered to vote.
- By 1905, that number had dropped to fewer than 1300 or less than one per cent of eligible black voters.
- Similar drops occurred in the other ten southern states that had comprised the original Confederacy.

The US Supreme Court denied any and all challenges to the altering of state constitutions because race was not specifically mentioned in the restriction of citizens from exercising the rights. Therefore, there was no violation of the 14th and 15th Amendments to the US Constitution. During the first half of the twentieth century, a number of lawsuits brought by the NAACP chipped away at the gross violation of African Americans' civil rights.

■ Methods used to deny the vote

The methods southern states used to deny African Americans the right to vote were ingenious and widespread. They included the following:

- **Poll tax**: citizens were required to pay a large sum in order to vote. This sum was difficult for many to pay, especially as it was sometimes cumulative. In other words, one had to pay the tax for all previous years in which one could have voted. In order that poor whites were not **disenfranchised**, the grandfather clause was introduced. If one's father or grandfather had voted prior to 1870, one could vote and not pay the poll tax. Because the vast majority of black people could not vote before 1870, the clause did not apply to them.
- Literacy and comprehension tests: in order to register to vote, black people were forced to take very difficult tests that supposedly measured either their literacy or ability to comprehend complex questions. Literacy tests were first used in Mississippi in 1890.
- Citizenship tests: these were similar to the literacy tests. Difficult questions on obscure state laws comprised the bulk of these exams.
- Property requirements: some states required that voters prove they had property worth a certain set amount. Most black people could not meet this requirement. White voters could vote under the grandfather clause.
- Intimidation: when black people did try to register to vote, they were often threatened with loss of their jobs or with violence.

Voting registrars were white and were the final judges on whether someone had answered questions on tests correctly. This also contributed to the tiny number of African Americans who were able to register to vote.

■ Political impact of disenfranchisement

The disenfranchisement of African Americans had political effects on the national government. By 1900, almost all southern representatives in **Congress** were members of the Democratic Party. This group of politicians represented a segregationist bloc of voters. They were able to stop any moves to desegregate the South until the 1950s and 1960s. Because the number of representatives is decided by the population of any given state and not by race, white southerners had a disproportionate number of Democratic congressmen. For example, in 1920, both Georgia and New Jersey had twelve representatives even though the number of voters in Georgia was 59,000 in contrast to the 338,000 voters in New Jersey.

The NAACP and other civil rights organizations increased their legal challenges to the system of disenfranchisement. Because black people did not have political power, they could not improve their lives. Being able to vote was the only way to change the inequality they faced every day. However, it would not be until the 1965 Voting Rights Act that literacy tests were banned and federal monitoring of voter registration took place.

IDENTIFYING RELEVANT CONTENT FROM AN ILLUSTRATION

- For Rights and protest Paper 1, questions are numbered from 13 to 16.
- The first question of Paper 1 contains two parts (13a and 13b), both of which test your understanding of two different sources.
- Question 13b is always a non-text source, that is, a political cartoon, propaganda poster, photograph, map or graph.
- Students are asked to identify two main messages or points from the source. The maximum value for 13b is 2 points.
- Students are asked to identify two main points from the source. Try to have at least two specific points in your answer. If you have made 3 points and one is incorrect, you will still score full (2) marks.
- When answering a question relating to a visual source, be sure to look closely at any words or dates on the visual. Are there any symbols that help in explaining the meaning of the source?

Examine the following illustration and then answer the following question that focuses on identifying relevant content.

SOURCE C

'By th' way, what's that big word?' An editorial cartoon by Bill Mauldin in 1962, first published in the *St. Louis Post-Dispatch* newspaper. Mauldin won a Pulitzer Prize for his incisive cartoons.

3   What does Source C suggest about literacy tests?

Segregation and education

Public school segregation

Nowhere in the segregated South were the differences between facilities for white and black people more stark than in the public school system. Although schools were supposed to be separate but equal, the reality was very different.

The majority of black people lived in rural areas. Children often did not attend school there because their labour was needed on farms. In cotton-growing areas, the school year was often tied to the growing and harvesting seasons. During those times, schools would be closed for all students.

Black versus white schools

Among the main differences between black and white schools were:

- Poor facilities: black schools often lacked bathrooms and electricity.
- Overcrowded conditions: class sizes in black schools were often double those in white schools.
- In many rural schools, all grades would be in one room.
- Supplies: black schools often relied on hand-me-down textbooks from white schools.
- Inferior quality of instruction: black teachers did not have as much training as their white counterparts. In some cases, teachers had not graduated from secondary school.
- Salaries: black teachers were only paid a fraction of white salaries.
- Curriculum: Jim Crow schools taught only those skills that were needed for farm and domestic work. Very few students went on to college.
- Funding: black schools received far less funding, such as in South Carolina where white schools received three times the amount as black schools.

Historically Black Colleges and Universities

The conditions at all-black colleges, known as Historically Black Colleges and Universities (HBCU), in the South were not much better. Many of these had been set up during and after Reconstruction and most were privately funded. This was because most white people did not want an educated black class that might challenge the gross inequalities in southern society, or to attend universities with white people.

- There were no colleges that offered degrees that led to a PhD.
- No institutions offered degrees in either engineering or architecture and only two offered programmes leading to a medical or law degree.
- Opportunities were certainly limited for those hoping to pursue professional careers.
- However, such civil rights leaders as Martin Luther King, Jr, Thurgood Marshall and Ida Wells Barnett did begin their academic careers at HBCUs.

James Meredith and the University of Mississippi

Those attempting to attend white universities faced huge challenges. In September 1962, James Meredith, a US Air Force veteran, entered the segregated University of Mississippi, after several rejected applications and a lawsuit. Over 150 law enforcement officials were on hand to protect Meredith. Over 3000 white segregationists rioted. Two civilians were killed and more than 300 injured in the street fighting.

EXAMINING THE CONTENT OF A SOURCE

- The second question of Paper 1 or question 14 requires students to evaluate the value and limitations of a source based on its origin, purpose and content.
- The origin of a source comes from several components: author, title, date of origin, type of source, and, if applicable, title, publisher and type of publication, and the country it originates from.
- Information about origin can be found in the description of a source that precedes the source's text.

The following questions are designed to make connections between the components of a source's origin and how they affect value or limitation. You can use the table following the questions to help you answer them.

SOURCE D

Extract from a 1985 interview with Melba Pattillo Beals, one of the original students to attend the all-white Central High School in Little Rock, Arkansas in 1957. The interview was included in the six-part documentary *Eyes on the Prize: America's Civil Rights Years, 1954–1963*. It was first broadcast in 1987.

Little Rock was separated, my world was for the most part black. Part of my family is white, my first cousins, etc. and those people I would go to town with occasionally, do things with, but for the most part my world was black. I went to a black high school called, uh, First Horseman, and then, uh, I just went to school every day. My mother was a school teacher, I uh, lived with my grandmother. … And going on rides on Sunday with my mother and we'd go past always Central High School, because it was a castle, looked like a castle and I always what was inside of it. … I wanted to go because they had more privileges. They had more equipment, they had five floors of opportunities. For me, I understood education before I understood anything else. From the time I was two, my mother said, 'You will go to college. Education is your key to survival,' and I understood that. And it was a kind of curiosity. It was not an overwhelming desire to go to this school and integrate this school and change history. … There was just, be, fun to go to this school I ride by everyday, I want to know what's in there. I don't necessarily want to be with those people, I assumed that being with those people would be no different than being with the people I was already with. I had no idea, none whatsoever, until the adventure started that it would be this way. And my getting into Central High School was somewhat almost of an accident. I simply raised my hand one day when they said, 'Who of you lives in the area of Central High School?' Then, that was two years before, in 1955, and um, they said, you know who has good grades, and I had excellent grades.

4   What is the origin of this source?
5   How is the origin helpful for historians studying segregated schools in the South?
6   What limitations might there be for the origin of this source?

	Key information	Limitations
Author		
Title		
Date published		
Type of source		
Publisher information		
Country of origin		

Brown v. Board of Education of Topeka decision (1954)

Role of the NAACP

The NAACP attempted to remove segregated facilities using legal means. The NAACP brought legal cases against a variety of state and local institutions that followed the discredited 'separate but equal' doctrine.

In 1950, Thurgood Marshall, the head of the NAACP Legal Fund, argued two cases in the Supreme Court. In *Sweatt v. Painter* and *McLaurin v. Oklahoma State Regents*, the Supreme Court overturned lower court decisions that had prevented black students from attending white-only graduate and professional schools.

The NAACP now turned its attention to public education, a much larger target than university graduate schools. Twenty-one southern and border states and the District of Columbia practised school segregation. In 1952, Marshall and the NAACP brought five cases to the Supreme Court all dealing with segregated public schools in the South. The first of these was *Brown v. Board of Education of Topeka*, named after the father of Linda Brown, an eight year old, who was forced to attend an all-black school on the other side of Topeka where she lived.

Supreme Court decision

It took the Supreme Court more than a year to reach its unanimous decision on 17 May 1954. Chief Justice Earl Warren ruled that:

- Segregated schools had a detrimental impact on the educational and personal growth of African American children.
- Segregated schools violated the Equal Protection Clause of the 14th Amendment of the Constitution.
- Racial segregation in schools was 'inherently unequal' and therefore unconstitutional.

White response to Supreme Court decision

The response was immediate. For white segregationists, the day was, as a US congressman from Mississippi declared in the House of Representatives, Black Monday. The NAACP and other civil rights groups hailed the decision as the first step in dismantling the unequal school systems.

Brown II

While the decision marked a significant legal victory for the forces of desegregation, many public schools in the South resisted the ruling. In the following year, the Supreme Court ruled on another lawsuit, named *Brown v. Board of Education of Topeka II* or simply *Brown II*. Southern states had asked the court to exempt them from desegregation. Warren issued the court's unanimous decision in this case, as well. He ruled that:

- Racial discrimination in public schools was unconstitutional.
- Local school boards would be responsible for desegregation.
- Federal courts were to oversee the process and to make sure the local authorities were acting in good faith.
- The process should be carried out with 'all deliberate speed'.

It was the fourth item that proved the most problematic since with 'all deliberate speed' was open to a wide range of interpretation. States could take as little or as much time as they thought necessary to desegregate their schools.

EXAMINING THE CONTENT OF A SOURCE

- Content refers to the information contained in a source.
- The content's value comes from information in the source that ties into the topic being examined.
- The content's limitations can come from information found in the source that addresses only part of the topic being examined.

For the question below, refer to Source E. The following question is designed to make connections between the content of a source and how it affects value or limitations. You can use the table below to help you formulate your answer.

SOURCE E

Extract from the NAACP's 'The Atlanta Declaration'. This was issued on 24 May.

All Americans are now relieved to have the law of the land declare in the clearest language: '… in the field of public education the doctrine of "separate but equal" has no place. Separate educational facilities are inherently unequal.' Segregation in public education is now not only unlawful; it is un-American. True Americans are grateful for this decision. Now that the law is made clear, we look to the future. Having canvassed the situation in each of our States, we approach the future with the utmost confidence. This confidence is based upon the many factors including the pledges of support and compliance by governors, attorney generals, mayors, and education officials; and by enlightened guidance of newspapers, radio, television and other organs of public communication and comment.

We stand ready to work with other law-abiding citizens who are anxious to translate this decision into a program of action to eradicate racial segregation in public education as speedily as possible … .

We look upon this memorable decision not as a victory for Negroes alone, but for the whole American people and as a vindication of America's leadership of the free world.

7   With reference to its content, analyse the value and limitations of Source E for historians studying the Supreme Court's *Brown v. Board of Education of Topeka* decision.

	Key information	Value	Limitations
Content			

Massive resistance

Reaction to *Brown I* and *II*: massive resistance

Because it remained unclear what exactly the Brown decision meant for segregated schools, the initial white southern response was muted. This would soon change, especially in the more rural areas of Mississippi and Alabama. In response to what was seen as an attack on white privilege, the first White Citizens' Council (WCC) was founded in Indianola, Mississippi in 1954. Many chapters of this racist organization soon appeared throughout the Deep South. Within two years, the WCC could count on perhaps 250,000 members. The members tended to be more middle and upper class than the secretive KKK ones and did not hide behind white sheets. Among the tactics employed to attack the growing Civil Rights Movement were:

- Economic retaliation. Black people were fired from their jobs or evicted from their rental homes. Loans were denied to them and their businesses were boycotted.
- Violence. Murders, lynchings, rapes and arson were used to create fear.
- Political activism. In some states, the WCC exerted great political power. In several Deep South states, many politicians were members of the group. In Mississippi, the WCC was supported with taxpayers' money. In Louisiana in 1956, a law was passed that segregated almost every aspect of public life.
- The promotion of 'council schools'. These private whites-only schools were created where school systems had chosen to integrate.

The KKK experienced a period of revival after the *Brown* ruling. Although the violent acts carried out by the Klan were often condemned, they assisted in the overall goal of stopping desegregation. When Klansmen were caught after a murder or fire-bombing of a church or home, they rarely were found guilty as they faced all-white juries.

Virginia Senator Harry Byrd, Sr called for 'massive resistance' to defend segregation. The state legislature passed a resolution in 1956 that declared that Virginia would not obey Supreme Court decisions it viewed as violating the state's sovereignty. Schools that admitted black students would be deprived of state funds. Other laws were passed to 'prevent a single Negro child from entering any white school'. Many public schools closed rather than integrate and public tuition grants were provided to students in order to attend whites-only 'segregation academies'.

Byrd was also key in persuading other southern congressmen to sign the Declaration of Constitutional Principles, better known as the Southern Manifesto, a call for the South to resist desegregation. The manifesto was signed by 101 of the 128 senators and representatives from the former states of the Confederacy in March 1956. The document included the following:

- a condemnation of the Supreme Court *Brown* and *Brown II* decisions
- a call to resist forced integration by any legal means
- a claim that the Supreme Court 'is destroying the amicable relations between the white and Negro races that have been created through 90 years of patient effort by the good people of both races. It has planted hatred and suspicion where there has been heretofore friendship and understanding.'

The overwhelming majority of southern white people opposed the *Brown* rulings, although opinion was not uniform. In the Deep South, the rate of opposition was 90% of white people, while in Texas the percentage was closer to 75%. Similarly, the Congressmen who most supported the Southern Manifesto were from the five Deep South states.

EXAMINING THE PURPOSE OF A SOURCE

- The purpose of a source is usually indicated by the source's title, the type of source, the writer or speaker, if it is a speech, or the location of the source, such as in a newspaper, an academic book or a journal.
- Sources can range from speeches that try to convince certain groups or nations that what the speaker is saying is the truth or should be heeded.

Read the following source and then answer the question.

SOURCE F

On 11 March, 1956, nineteen Senators and 82 Congressmen signed a resolution they called the 'Southern Manifesto'. All were from Southern states. Extract from the *Congressional Record, 84th Congress Second Session*, Vol. 102, part 4. Governmental Printing Office, Washington, DC, 1956, pages 4459–60.

… We regard the decision of the Supreme Court in the school cases as a clear abuse of judicial power. It climaxes a trend in the federal judiciary undertaking to legislate, in derogation of the authority of Congress, and to encroach upon the reserved rights of the states and the people.

The original Constitution does not mention education. Neither does the Fourteenth Amendment nor any other amendment. The debates preceding the submission of the Fourteenth Amendment clearly show that there was no intent that it should affect the systems of education maintained by the states … .

This unwarranted exercise of power by the court, contrary to the Constitution, is creating chaos and confusion in the states principally affected. It is destroying the amicable relations between the white and Negro races that have been created through 90 years of patient effort by the good people of both races. It has planted hatred and suspicion where there has been heretofore friendship and understanding.

Without regard to the consent of the governed, outside agitators are threatening immediate and revolutionary changes in our public school systems. If done, this is certain to destroy the system of public education in some of the states.

With the gravest concern for the explosive and dangerous condition created by this decision and inflamed by outside meddlers: We reaffirm our reliance on the Constitution as the fundamental law of the land … .

8   With reference to its purpose, analyse the value and limitations of Source F for historians studying the white southern reaction to *Brown v. Board of Education*. You can fill in the table below to help understand the purpose of the source:

Source's title	
Type of source	
Writer/speaker	
Location	

Little Rock (1957)

■ Desegregation at Central High School, Little Rock, Arkansas

The crisis over desegregation of schools reached a crisis point in Little Rock, Arkansas in 1957.

Nine African Americans students requested admittance to the all-white Central High School. The students would soon become known as the Little Rock Nine. The six girls and three boys had been carefully vetted by the Arkansas branch of the NAACP. The NAACP wanted students who had the strength of character to be able to withstand what was sure to be continual harassment and both verbal and physical attacks.

■ Timeline of Little Rock events

The following timeline explains the sequence of events in Little Rock:

- 2 September 1957. Arkansas Governor Orval Faubus said he would call in the Arkansas National Guard to stop the nine students from entering the school.
- 2 September. A federal judge ruled that desegregation would take place on the opening day of school.
- 4 September. Eight of the nine students arrived at the school together. The ninth, Elizabeth Eckford, did not get the message that the students would be taken to Central High by carpool because her family did not have a phone. Eckford bore the brunt of the insults that day. Photographs of her walking to the school building alone while a furious mob insulted her were published worldwide. The nine students were not allowed entrance to the school.
- 23 September. The Little Rock Nine entered the school unnoticed by a mob of over 1000 whites. Parents attempted to enter the school to attack the students. In a rapidly deteriorating situation, the police removed the nine students from Central High for their own safety.
- 24 September. President Eisenhower ordered 1200 members of the US Army's 101st Airborne Division to Little Rock. Another 1000 members of the Arkansas National Guard were federalized.
- 25 September. The Little Rock Nine entered Central High for their first full day of classes.
- September 1958. The Supreme Court decided unanimously in *Cooper v. Aaron* that states must abide by the court's decisions. In regard to Little Rock, this meant that the schools must desegregate.
- September 1958. Governor Faubus closed all four Little Rock high schools for one year after 80% of voters chose not to desegregate their schools in a public referendum. This became known as the 'Lost Year'.
- September 1959. Schools reopened. African American students were allowed in.

■ Treatment of the Little Rock Nine

During the 1957–8 school year, the Little Rock Nine suffered untold incidents of abuse. One student, Minnijean Brown, struck back at her attackers and was expelled. One hundred white students were suspended at different times during the year and four expelled for their actions against the nine. The Airborne soldiers were withdrawn after two months but the National Guardsmen remained for the whole academic year. Ernest Green became the first African American to graduate from Central High. Several of the others would do so in 1960.

■ White reaction to desegregation

Besides the state government's attempts to stop the integration of public schools, two groups also helped foster racial hatred in Little Rock. The Capital Citizens' Council, a local chapter of the White Citizens' Council, issued dire warnings of what might happen because of racial mixing. It also pushed the claim that there was a link between the NAACP and international communism. Assisting the council was the Mothers' League of Central High School. It tried to provide a 'feminine' perspective to the segregation movement.

While the Little Rock crisis did demonstrate that the federal government was willing to act forcefully to force integration, progress was slow. By 1964, fewer than two per cent of African American children attended formerly all-white public schools.

ANALYSING THE VALUE AND LIMITATIONS OF A SOURCE WITH REFERENCE TO ITS ORIGIN, PURPOSE AND CONTENT

- Now that you have looked at the value and limitations of a source through its origin, purpose and content separately, it is time to put the three of them together in one answer.
- Question 14 will ask you to do so. The value of this question is 4 marks. It is fine to write your answer in three separate parts: the value and limitations of the origin, purpose and content.

Read the following source closely and then answer the question. You can use the table below the source to help you formulate your answer.

SOURCE G

Extract from the 1962 book *The Long Shadow of Little Rock* written by Daily Bates. Bates was the president of the Arkansas NAACP and editor-in-chief of the black newspaper the *Arkansas State Press*. Quoted in Clayborne Carson, ed., *The Eyes on the Prize Civil Rights Reader*, Penguin Books, New York, 1991, page 98.

I don't recall all the details of what Governor Faubus said that night. But his words electrified Little Rock. By morning they shocked the United States. By noon the next day his message horrified the world.

Faubus' alleged reason for calling out the troops was that he had received information that caravans of automobiles filled with white supremacists were heading toward Little Rock from all over the states. He therefore declared Central High School off limits to Negroes …

Then, from the chair of the highest office of the State of Arkansas, Governor Orval Eugene Faubus delivered the infamous words, 'blood will run in the streets' if Negro pupils should attempt to enter Central High School.

In a half dozen ill-chosen words, Faubus made his contribution to the mass hysteria that was to grip the city of Little Rock for several months.

The citizens of Little Rock gathered on September 3 to gaze upon the incredible spectacle of an empty school building surrounded by 250 National Guard troops. At eight fifteen in the morning, Central students started passing through the line of national guardsmen – all but the nine Negro students.

I had been in touch with their parents throughout the day. They were confused, and they were frightened. As the parents voiced their fears, they kept repeating Faubus' words that 'blood would run in the streets of Little Rock' should their teenage children try to attend Central – the school to which they had been assigned by the school board.

9   With reference to its origin, purpose and content, analyse the value and limitations of Source G for historians studying the desegregation of schools in the South.

	Key information	Value	Limitations
Origin			
Purpose			
Content			

Economic and social discrimination

Revised

■ Jim Crow

The Jim Crow era refers to a period that roughly spanned the years from 1881 to 1964. The Supreme Court decision in *Plessy v. Ferguson* in 1896 ended the early challenges to legal segregation. The Supreme Court ruled that separating white and black people was legal as long as the separate facilities were equal. Before long, Americans were separated by racial laws in 26 states. Most of the southern states practised *de jure* segregation or legal separation. A whole series of state, county and local statutes were created to separate the races by law. In other states, legal means were not employed to achieve this end; long-standing traditions or codes of conduct were enough to ensure segregation. This was known as *de facto* segregation. Whether by law or custom, separate facilities were certainly not equal.

■ Social impact of the Jim Crow laws

Virtually every aspect of daily life was segregated, from the use of public parks and libraries to where one could eat or go to the toilet. White people hoped to maintain their superior position over black people and reacted often violently to any threats to the *status quo*. The right to vote was severely restricted for black people throughout the South. It was miscegenation that seemed to be the most dangerous idea and this was not just true in the South. Thirty-eight states outlawed marriage between white and black people. In the case of segregated schools, even President Eisenhower weighed in when he told the Chief Justice of the Supreme Court that, 'These [white southerners] are not bad people. All they are concerned about is to see that their sweet little girls are not required to sit in schools alongside some big black bucks.'

■ Examples of the extent of Jim Crow laws

The scope of the laws was astounding. Here is a brief selection of laws which illustrates the length to which white people went to keep the races apart:

- Louisiana: a law separated white and black blind people in state institutions.
- Mississippi: every hospital needed separate entrances for white and black patients and visitors.
- Alabama: no white female nurse could work in a room in which black men were placed.
- Virginia: trains must have separate cars for the races.
- Texas: coal mines were required to have separate washrooms.
- Tennessee: there were separate buildings for white and black patients in hospitals for the insane.
- Kentucky: all parks, recreation centres and playgrounds were required to be separated.
- Georgia: 'It shall be unlawful for any amateur white baseball team to play baseball on any vacant lot or baseball diamond within two blocks of a playground devoted to the Negro race.'
- South Carolina: a white person could not make a black person the guardian or adopted parents of a white child.
- North Carolina: 'Books shall not be interchangeable between the white and colored [black] schools, but shall continue to be used by the race first using them.'

COMPARING TWO SOURCES

- As you read the following two sources, fill in the chart below listing how each is similar to the other.
- You should be able to come up with at least three comparisons.

Similarity 1	
Similarity 2	
Similarity 3	

SOURCE H

Extract from Ruth Thompson-Miller, Joe Feagin and Leslie Picca, *Jim Crow's Legacy: The Lasting Impact of Segregation*, Rowman & Littlefield, Lanham, Maryland, 2014, page 51. Dolores Arnold was interviewed by the authors when she was in her seventies.

And like I said, my first child was, [I was] pregnant. We was in Atlanta, and I had to ride the bus to New Orleans. And they could have fifty dozen seats empty up front, you didn't sit down, you sit in the back. They didn't care if you're pregnant as big as a house, you were black, so you sit in the back. That's why I don't too much trust white folks. I don't. I don't respect them, 'cause they didn't nothing about you, you know. Like I said my grandfather was white and black, and you couldn't tell he wasn't white. You know what I'm saying? But that don't mean nothing to them. They don't care. If you got a little bit of color in you, you black. A 'nigger', that's what they call you. Negroes was 'niggerous' women … . 'Nigger, what you want?' You know that's the way it was. I am serious! And when I'm at the nursing home, and I be running my mouth I can see them old white ones in there saying, 'She must think she's something.' Don't say nothing to me, 'cause you might get hit! Yep. [She laughs]. Yes.

SOURCE I

The following is also drawn from *Jim Crow's Legacy: The Lasting Impact of Segregation*, page 42. Roy Turner was interviewed when he was in his seventies.

I served in the army. There was time when they sent me from Oklahoma to El Paso [Texas]. Back then, you couldn't go in a place to eat. We started riding about, during that whole trip they stopped about three times to eat, but uh, the driver came up to me and said, 'Man, I'm sorry, but you can't some in this place to eat, I'll bring you something.' I said, 'Never mind, if they don't want me to eat I just won't eat.' So we made a second stop, he said the same thing. Early in the morning, about 5:00 we go over there into Mexico. He say, when we get over into Mexico, I could stop and get out. Ain't that something? All the white folks is eating, but the Negro can starve to death. And that's when I ate.

Source booklet

Read Sources M and N below and answer questions 13a and 13b in the accompanying question paper.

SOURCE M

Governor Barnett's Declaration to the People of Mississippi. This was broadcast via television and radio on 13 September 1962. Barnett was trying to block the court-ordered admission of James Meredith to the all-white University of Mississippi. The complete speech can be found at: http:// microsites.jfklibrary.org/olemiss/controversy/doc2.html

Ladies and gentlemen, my friends and fellow Mississippians: I speak to you as your Governor in a solemn hour in the history of our great state and in our nation's history. I speak to you now in the moment of our greatest crisis since the War Between the States.

In the absence of constitutional authority and without legislative action, an ambitious federal government, employing naked and arbitrary power, has decided to deny us the right of self-determination in the conduct of the affairs of our sovereign state. Having long since failed in their efforts to conquer the indomitable spirit of the people of Mississippi and their unshakable will to preserve the sovereignty and majesty of our commonwealth, they now seek to break us physically with the power of force.

Even now as I speak to you tonight, professional agitators and the unfriendly liberal press and other trouble makers are pouring across our borders intent upon instigating strife among our people. Paid propagandists are continually hammering away at us in the hope that they can succeed in bringing about a division among us. Every effort is being made to intimidate us into submission to the tyranny of judicial oppression. The Kennedy Administration is lending the power of the federal government to the ruthless demands of these agitators. Thus we see our own federal government teamed up with a motley array of un-American pressure groups against us. This is the crisis we face today …

SOURCE N

'And you incited those innocent rioters to violence.' This political cartoon was created by Bill Mauldin. It was published on 29 November 1962 in the *Chicago Sun Times*. It refers to the judicial aftermath of a huge riot in Oxford, Mississippi in September 1962 when protesters tried to stop James Meredith from entering the University of Mississippi. Meredith was protected by US marshals. Two rioters were killed and many others, including US marshals, were injured.

Sample questions and answers

Below are sample answers. Read them and the comments around them.

- Question 13 of Paper 1 contains two parts, both of which test understanding of two different sources.
- Question 13a always refers to a narrative excerpt. Students are asked to identify main points from the source. This part of the question is worth 3 marks. That means three main points must be identified. Do not go into too much detail. List at least three main points. **Note:** the phrase 'main points' means important understandings from the source. It **does not** mean simply listing facts from the source.
- Question 13b is a non-narrative text, usually an illustration of some type. Students are asked to identify the message of the source. This part of the question is worth 2 marks. Do not spend too much time on the response. List at least two messages from the source. Two sentences are enough to fulfil the demands of this question.
- The two parts of question 13 should take about five minutes to answer.

13a According to Source M, what were the dangers facing Mississippi?

> Mississippi faced several dangers. The federal government was abusing its authority and violating the rights of Mississippi by intervening in a state matter. Furthermore, outsiders and member of the 'liberal press' were flooding the state. These groups tried to divide the people with their lies. Finally, the federal government was helping the anti-American outsiders to work against Mississippi.

Understand what the question asks you to do, also known as the demands of the question. In this case you are to determine the dangers facing Mississippi, according to the governor.

3/3. The response indicates that the student read and understood what the source stated. The response includes three main points. The question is answered in paragraph form and not bullet points. The answer repeats part of the question, using the phrase, 'Mississippi faced several dangers'. The response paraphrases the three main points.

13b What does the cartoon suggest about Mississippi's judicial system?

> The cartoon suggests that Mississippi's judicial system was corrupt because the judge is blaming the US marshal for hurting rioters. He even goes so far as to claim that the rioters would not have turned to violence if they had not been encouraged by the marshals.

Understand what the question asks you to do. When examining a cartoon, be sure to pay close attention to any words. In this cartoon, Mississippi's judicial system is represented by the words 'MISSISSIPPI GRAND JURY.' The judge tells the obviously injured US marshal, 'AND YOU INCITED THOSE INNOCENT RIOTERS TO VIOLENCE'. This cartoon suggests the opposite to be true but that Mississippi would blame the innocent and protect the guilty.

2/2. The response clearly states two observations about the cartoon. The question is answered in sentences and not bullet points. The response begins by using the phrasing of the question so that it is focused on the demands of the question.

Exam practice

Now it's your turn to take a mock exam.

Read Sources M–P below and answer questions 13–16 in the accompanying question paper. The sources and questions relate to Case study 1: The Civil Rights Movement in the United States 1954–65 – nature and characteristics of discrimination: segregation and education; Little Rock (1957).

SOURCE M

Relman Morin was a US journalist who wrote for the Associated Press wire service. He received a Pulitzer Prize for his Little Rock reporting. His story 'Violence at Central High' was published on 23 September, 1957. Quoted in Clayborne Carson, ed., *Reporting Civil Rights, Part One*, Library of America, New York, 2013.

At that instant, the eight Negroes – the three boys and five girls – were crossing the schoolyard toward a side door at the south end of the school. The girls were in bobby sox and the boys were dressed in shirts open at the neck. All were carrying books.

They were not running, not even walking fast. They simply strolled toward the steps, went up and were inside before all but a few of the two hundred people at the end of the street knew it.

'They're going in,' a man roared. 'Oh, God, the niggers are in the school.'

A woman screamed, 'Did they get in? Did you see them go in?'

'They're in now,' some other men yelled.

'Oh, my God,' the woman screamed. She burst into tears and tore at her hair. Hysteria swept the crowd. Other women began weeping and screaming … .

Suddenly, another roar – and cheering and clapping – came from the crowd. A white student, carrying his books, came down from the steps. He was followed by two girls wearing bobby sox. In the next few minutes, other students came out. Between 15 and 20 left the school within the next half hour.

Each time they appeared, the people clapped and cheered. 'Come on out,' they yelled. 'Don't stay in there with the niggers. Go back and tell all of them to come out.'

SOURCE N

Nackey Loeb drew this editorial cartoon for her husband's newspaper, the *Manchester Union Leader*, a conservative newspaper in New Hampshire. It was published on 26 September 1957. New Hampshire is a northern state.

"Start loving each other. That's a court order!"

SOURCE O

A 1985 interview with Melba Pattillo Beals, one of the Little Rock Nine students, Washington University Libraries.

The first day uh, that we went to school, the kind of things that I endured were [white] parents got in the school, and parents were kicking, parents were hitting, parents were throwing things. Uh, you would get tripped, people would just walk up and hit you in the face. And you couldn't hit back, we'd been instructed by this time that any attempts to hit back to respond, to call a name in response would mean the end of the case. So, by now we were savvy warriors, we were beginning the journey towards becoming the warrior that would make the trip through Central High School. … And you know, anything that was possible to happen, did happen. … this is the first day we go in without the troops. So the, the greatest feeling I had was one of a lack of protection. There was nobody to resort to. There was no help, there was no one on my side, I was on my side. And the only way to get through it was to count on myself …

The next time I went to Central High School, I was escorted by the 101 Airborne Division … and they were in uniform. I went in a jeep; there was a jeep behind me with a [gap] gun and one in front. Actually, we were in a station wagon, there were two jeeps accompanying us, and there were helicopters overhead. And uh, I went in not through the side doors, but up the front stairs, and there was a feeling of pride and hope that yes, this is the United States, yes there is a reason I salute the flag, and it's going to be O.K., you know. These guys go with us the first time, it [*sic*] going to be O.K. … And kids would do things like, in the study hall in particular, walk by and drop a lighted piece of paper on your books. We changed books as much as 3 or 4 times a week. You go to your locker and there would be ink all over everything you own. I was walking down a hall one day with my personal guards name was Johnny Black at the time, and somebody, I think I anyway somebody spewed acid in my eye. They walked up with a water gun, they do that often, and you'd expect water, that'd be cool, this time I got acid in my eyes and everything went flying and I had long hair and he took my braid and slammed my head beneath the water faucet.

SOURCE P

Extract from David Nichols, *A Matter of Justice: Eisenhower and the Beginning of the Civil Rights Revolution*, Simon & Schuster, New York, 2007, pages 189–90. Nichols is a US historian specializing in President Eisenhower.

That morning chaos reigned at Central High School. A mob gathered, determined to keep the African-American students from entering the school. A newsman reported: 'This was a mob with a job to do and the leadership to do it.' The men were dressed in gray and khaki work clothes, straw hats and work shoes; obvious ringleaders were organizing the crowd. One was Jimmy Karma, the state athletic commissioner and close associate of Governor Faubus …

At the south side of the school, the crowd intercepted four Negro newsmen. A white man stopped them: 'You're not going into our school.' The reporters replied that they did not wish to enter. A mob leader called out: 'Kill them, kill them!' Several men beat two of the reporters. During the melee, eight of the Negro students slipped through a side door of the school. A woman saw them: 'Oh, my god, they're going in. The niggers are in.' She fell to her knees and covered her face …

The riot continued for more than three hours. … Eventually, the crowd broke through the police barricades surrounding the school and the police removed the students from the school for their own protection.

13 a Why, according to Source O, was the presence of 101 Airborne Division paratroopers very important? [3]

   b What does Source N suggest about desegregation? [2]

14 With reference to its origin, purpose and content, analyse the value and limitations of Source O for a historian studying school desegregation in 1957. [4]

15 Compare and contrast how Sources M and P describe desegregation at Central High School in Little Rock, Arkansas. [6]

16 Using the sources and your own knowledge, evaluate the racial divisions in the USA in 1957. [9]

2 Protests and action

Montgomery Bus Boycott

■ Rosa Parks

The Montgomery Bus Boycott is probably the best-known event in the Civil Rights Movement.

Montgomery, Alabama was a deeply segregated city. Black people were forced to sit in the back of public buses. One-third of the population was black.

On 1 December 1955, Rosa Parks boarded a bus and sat behind the driver. When the bus filled up, the driver told her to give up her seat to a white man. She refused and was arrested.

Rosa Parks' possible motivations:

- She had been moved by the story of Emmett Till, a fourteen-year-old boy who had been brutally beaten to death in Mississippi for supposedly whistling at a white woman. His murderers were acquitted of all charges. The case outraged people throughout the USA.
- She was an active member of the Montgomery branch of the NAACP. She had often complained about the treatment blacks received on the city's public buses.
- She knew that her actions would result in her arrest. She was not the first to have refused to give up her seat. In an earlier incident, a young girl had been arrested. However, because she was pregnant and unmarried, the NAACP decided not to publicize the case. Parks, on the other hand, was a respectable, dignified, married woman.

■ The boycott

Black people in Montgomery were encouraged by local leaders such as E.D. Nixon and Jo Ann Robinson to boycott public transport on the day of Parks' trial, 5 December 1955, only four days after the arrest of Parks. Through meetings, especially ones held in churches, the black community was organized. Because the majority of the bus riders were black, a boycott would hurt the bus company's white owners.

■ Montgomery Improvement Association

Almost all of the 40,000 African American riders boycotted the buses. It soon became clear that in order to force the company to treat them more civilly, the boycott would have to be extended. Nixon called a meeting of 50 church ministers, the most influential leaders of the community, and they set up the Montgomery Improvement Association (MIA) to organize the boycott. The MIA invited a young Baptist minister, Dr Martin Luther King, Jr, to be president of the group. He delivered a stirring message to a large crowd of 5000 on the evening of the first day of the boycott.

At the meeting, three objectives for the boycott were agreed on:

- Black passengers should be treated more courteously.
- Seating would be on a first-come, first-served basis with white people filling the bus from the front and black people from the back.
- Black drivers should be employed.

■ Mass mobilization

The boycotters at first did not demand that the Montgomery buses should be desegregated. In response, the bus company refused to compromise in any way. Most whites thought the black people would not be able to organize a sustained and organized campaign. They were proven wrong:

- For 381 days, the black citizens of Montgomery walked and cycled to work and rode in cheap carpools and in black-owned taxis.
- They were encouraged by their ministers to resist and their spirits were kept up at mass meetings.
- Mass meetings were held to keep people unified and mobilized.

READING FOR COMPREHENSION

Read Source A closely, keeping in mind the following question: What evidence is there in Source A that African American bus riders in Montgomery might find objectionable?

Now answer the question in one paragraph. Try to raise at least three distinct points in your answer.

SOURCE A

Extract from *Code of the City of Montgomery, Alabama*. Michie City Publishing Co., Charlottesville, 1952. Alabama Department of Archives and History, Montgomery, Alabama.

Sec. 10. Separation of races – Required. Every person operating a bus line in the city shall provide equal but separate accommodations for white people and negroes on his buses, by requiring the employees in charge thereof to assign passengers seats on the vehicles under their charge in such manner as to separate the white people from the negroes, where there are both white and negroes on the same car; provided, however, that negro nurses having in charge white children or sick or infirm white persons, may be assigned seats among white people.

Nothing in this section shall be construed as prohibiting the operators of such bus lines from separating the races by means of separate vehicles if they see fit. (Code 1938, §§603, 606.)

Sec. 11. Same – Powers of persons in charge of vehicle; passengers to obey directions. Any employee in charge of a bus operated in the city shall have the powers of a police officer of the city while in actual charge of any bus, for the purpose of carrying out the provisions of the preceding section, and it shall be unlawful for any passenger to refuse or fail to take a seat among those assigned to the race to which he belongs, at the request of any such employee in charge, if there is such a seat vacant. (Code 1938, §604.)

Sec. 12. Failure to carry passengers. It shall be unlawful for any person operating a bus line in the city to refuse, without sufficient excuse, to carry any passenger; provided that no driver of a bus shall be required to carry any passenger who is intoxicated or disorderly, or who is afflicted with any contagious or infectious disease, or who refuses to pay in advance the fare required, or who for any other reason deemed satisfactory by the recorder should be excluded. (Code 1938, §§699.)

1   What evidence is there in Source A that African American bus riders in Montgomery might find objectionable?

■ Results of the boycott

■ Initial results of the boycott

Dr King's house was fire-bombed in January 1956. The white supremacists thought they could intimidate King and other boycott leaders, but they were greatly mistaken. King became a hero for standing up to them and by preaching non-violence in the face of attacks.

Because of the attacks on black leaders and the arrests of several church leaders, huge publicity was attracted to the bus boycott both nationally and internationally. Donations poured in and cars were purchased for the carpool to help ferry black people to work.

In June 1956, the MIA agreed to challenge the segregation laws in a federal court:

- Thurgood Marshall and the NAACP lent their legal expertise to the case.
- The federal court ruled that the bus company's system of forcing blacks to sit in the rear of the bus was unconstitutional.
- The court ruled that the bus company had violated the 14th Amendment, which guaranteed 'equal protection of the laws' for all citizens.
- Montgomery appealed the verdict to the Supreme Court.
- On 20 December 1956, the court upheld the lower court's decision.
- The bus company was forced to back down.
- The leaders of the boycott, including King and Nixon, rode on the first desegregated bus in Montgomery.

■ The success of the boycott

The reasons the boycott was successful included the following:

- Black unity in the face of intimidation and terror was firm.
- Confidence and pride made people more determined to continue their campaign.
- The use of economic power as a weapon could achieve results against the white establishment.
- Organized and collective action was a powerful unifying force.
- Dr King became a potent symbol of the struggle. He helped unify groups in Montgomery and won respect for the movement far beyond Alabama. His non-violent message appealed to many across the nation.
- Churches became the organizing centres for the boycott. They lent further legitimacy to the boycott since they played a central role in the black community.

The bus boycott was, according to some, the psychological turning point in the Civil Rights Movement. The black church became the focal point of organizing the fight for equal rights and many participants in the long boycott lost their fear of the white, ruling establishment.

COMPARING AND CONTRASTING SOURCES

- When asked to compare and contrast two sources, it is important to keep in mind that you should focus on the content of each source and not its author or its origin.
- Focus on the ideas raised in each source. Answer the question after Source C. Try to come up with three similarities and three contrasts. If this is not possible, a split of four and two would also be acceptable.

SOURCE B

Extract from Stuart Burns, ed., *Daybreak of Freedom: The Montgomery Bus Boycott*, University of North Carolina Press, Chapel Hill, 1997, pages xii–xiii. Burns is an American professor of History at Stanford University.

Montgomery showed that democracy cannot bloom without community. The richer the communal soil, the stronger its democratic shoots. The bus boycott exemplified an unparalleled unity across class lines that black movements have dreamt about since. The driving force of it all was thousands of African American women, middle class and working class, active in churches, clubs, and sororities. They transplanted democracy from their sheltered sanctuaries to public streets and squares. They turned faith and friendship from the healing balm of survival into the fire of defiance and transformation.

Blocked from voting by and large, lacking representation in the political arena, Montgomery's black citizens understood that, like their nineteenth-century forebears who fought slavery, democracy meant that they 'must themselves strike the blow'. They must act as their own agents of change. They came to believe, as their preeminent leader told them, that 'the great glory of democracy is the right to protest for right'.

SOURCE C

Roy Wilkins in *Liberation* magazine, December 1956. Quoted in Stuart Burns, ed., *Daybreak of Freedom: The Montgomery Bus Boycott*, University of North Carolina Press, Chapel Hill, 1997, page 315. In 1956, Wilkins was the executive secretary of the NAACP.

Long known as the first capital of the late Confederacy, the City of Montgomery, Alabama, now has a new and more righteous claim to fame. Once the war capital of an alliance dedicated to human slavery, it is now the peace capital of a new liberation movement. Formerly a more or less complacent Southern town, it has become a center of activity providing a demonstration of the effectiveness of non-violent resistance to racial tyranny.

The rebirth of Montgomery came with the spontaneous protest of the city's Negro population against the humiliation of Jim Crow. This upsurge of protest was channeled into constructive action by the Montgomery Improvement Association under the inspired and dedicated leadership of Martin Luther King Jr., Ralph Abernathy, and E.D. Nixon.

The Montgomery protest is an historic development. It demonstrates before all the world that Negroes have the capacity for sustained collective action. It refutes the white supremacist's false charge that Negroes are content with discrimination and segregation. It validates the role of local leadership in social action programs. It reveals the economic strength of the Negro. It affirms the value of a calm approach to potentially explosive issues. And finally, it demonstrates that 50,000 persons can work together as a unit without military discipline and without degenerating into a mob.

2   Compare and contrast how Sources B and C interpret the Montgomery Bus Boycott.

Non-violent protests: sit-ins

■ First sit-in

On 1 February 1960, four black students from North Carolina A&T College sat down at the whites-only lunch counter at a Woolworth store in Greensboro, North Carolina. Service was refused them and they sat until the store closed. More students joined in the sit-ins over the next several days. Young white people attacked the peaceful and quiet protesters. Soon many were arrested for disorderly conduct even though they actually were anything but disorderly. The news of the sit-ins spread quickly and soon thousands of black and white students participated in similar sit-ins across the South. The Greensboro four had started a mass protest movement by their simple actions. In the North, protesters picketed Woolworth stores for continuing to refuse service to black people in the southern states.

■ The rise of sit-ins

By 1960, many young people were beginning to become frustrated by the lack of civil rights progress. Other reasons they turned to sit-ins included the following:

● In the six years since the *Brown* Supreme Court decision and *Brown II*, desegregation had failed to take hold in many areas of public life.
● In 1960, there were thirteen African countries that had become free of colonial rule. The southern states, in comparison, did not seem to offer the same freedoms.
● A new national Civil Rights Movement based on non-violent resistance was growing.
● Hundreds of thousands of African Americans began to boycott stores in the North and South that did not hire black workers but willingly took their money.

■ Nashville protests

One important new focal point of protests was Nashville, Tennessee. Here, students participated in workshops on civil disobedience and other black citizens began to boycott many of the major stores in the city. The well-organized non-violent students held sit-ins from 13 February until 10 May 1960:

● On 27 February, white opponents attacked sit-in protesters.
● Eighty-one protesters were arrested while none of the attackers were.
● The students refused to pay **bail** and the jails soon filled up with many more protesters.
● Many of the jailed students were released because there was no more room for them.
● The students held firm for full integration of the lunch counters in their negotiations with the mayor of Nashville.

On 19 April, the home of the attorney representing the students was destroyed in a bomb attack. It was at this juncture that the mayor appealed for calm in the face of more mass protests. He urged an end to discrimination and bigotry. Within several weeks, the major stores finally allowed blacks and whites to sit at the same lunch counters. It would still take another four years for other public businesses such as cinemas and restaurants to be fully integrated.

Woolworth stores desegregated all its food facilities within a year in the face of boycotts and sit-ins.

■ NAACP and SCLC reactions

The NAACP and the Southern Christian Leadership Conference (SCLC), the group headed by King, criticized the sit-ins. Both organizations wanted to pursue desegregation through the court system instead of through confrontation. Nonetheless, both groups offered students help with non-violence training and legal aid.

Out of the sit-in movement grew an important new civil rights group, the Student Nonviolent Coordinating Committee (SNCC), better known as 'Snick'. This group formed in April 1960 at the urging of the Ella Baker, a long-time rights' activist and executive director of the SCLC. Baker urged students to continue their activism and to target more than just lunch counters. Many young people joined this new group, which was independent of the more conservative SCLC and NAACP. SNCC would play an important role in some of the upcoming struggles.

ANALYSING MEMOIRS AND EYEWITNESS ACCOUNTS

Read the following two sources, both from the same participant of sit-ins, and then answer the questions that follow below.

Try to write at least one full paragraph in answer to each question.

SOURCE D

Extract from Merrill Proudfoot, *Diary of a Sit-In*, second edition, University of Illinois Press, Urbana, 1990, pages 53–4. The book was first published in 1962. Proudfoot was a white Presbyterian clergyman on the faculty of Knoxville College, a black college in Knoxville, Tennessee.

Monday, June 20 [1960]. At the ten o'clock meeting I reported the rules drawn up by our committee. We did not mimeograph them for fear they might fall into the hands of hostile persons …

'Demonstrators should not leave an establishment at the request of the manager alone, but will leave when requested by the police.

'In situations where management tries to exclude demonstrators while admitting other customers, we will send such a large delegation of demonstrators that when they stand in line in normal fashion it will be difficult for other customers to enter; we will not deliberately try to prevent their entry.'

We listed the objectives of the sit-ins in the following order of importance:

'1. To secure service on a non-discriminatory basis;

'2. To demonstrate that white customers will continue to patronize the establishment when Negroes are at the counter;

'3. To demonstrate to the management that more money would be made by serving all the people seated at his counter.' …

'Normally a Negro and a white demonstrator sill sit together with two vacant seats on either side of them.'

Several rules served to clamp a tight discipline on demonstrators:

'Each delegation should have an adult leader whose authority is recognized by every demonstrator. The leader should be a Negro.

'Demonstrators will stay in their seating facing the counter – no moving about in the store or from store to store.

'No knives or other sharp instruments, no smoking; men will not wear hats at the counter … .'

(We intended leaning over backward to avoid any appearance of toughness. We wanted our group to look better and behave better than anyone else at the counter.) …

Based on our experience of Friday, one rule provided that whenever a white demonstrator leaves a store, one or two Negro men should follow to protect him.

Finally, the non-violent nature of our protest was recognized in two simple rules: 'Demonstrators will ignore heckling, blows, and other attempts to provoke. Demonstrators will avoid caustic remarks.'

SOURCE E

Extract from Merrill Proudfoot, *Diary of a Sit-In*, second edition, University of Illinois Press, Urbana, 1990, pages 92–3.

Walgreen's is the only place we go that has booths; Logan and I occupy one together. A man in a white jacket who seems to be in charge of the counter manifests his hostility from the beginning. As he passes by our booth, he conspicuously spits on the floor. The next time he tosses a lighted cigaret [sic] on me; it rests in a fold of my coat. I would prefer to ignore it, but must pluck it off before it burns a hole in my good suit. I want to examine the coat to see if it is damaged, but I must not do anything here that will indicate anxiety. A young white fellow stops at our booth, inquires about Robert Booker, who he says he knows. Now I see him bring coffee which he has ordered to one of our Negro boys and a coke to another. I wish he had not done that. The demonstrators do not touch the drinks. Logan suggests the drinks may be drugged; I had not thought of that! The man in the white coat comes to pick up the drinks. He deliberately spills the coke over the demonstrator, and now the coffee, exclaiming with mock apology, 'Oh, excuse me!'

A woman customer brushes close to our booth and mutters to me, 'Take your niggers and get out of here!'

A group of what boys who appear to be high school age come up to our booth and begin to tantalize me. I do not recognize the fellow who heckled me before; these boys have a younger appearance, but their line is the same: 'Come on with us, fellow; we're going to show you where you belong!' …

As they continue their heckling, I look straight ahead at Logan. Suddenly I feel myself drenched with what seems a terrific lot of liquid. My glasses are filmed over; I take them off and hold them in my clenched hands. My eyes smart – what was the stuff? The liquid has gone down all over my 'preachin' suit'. … I can sense as though I had eyes all over my head that everyone in the establishment is looking at me; I feel I have the sympathy of most of them. Nevertheless, it is a mortifying experience to be attacked in public by another person and not be able to do anything in your own defense.

3   What are the limitations of these sources for historians studying the sit-ins?
4   How might these sources prove valuable for historians studying non-violent activism in the Civil Rights Movement?

Non-violent protests: Freedom Rides (1961)

Interstate travel and the law

Although there had been several Supreme Court decisions that desegregated interstate travel and restaurants in bus and rail terminals, the US government declined to enforce the law. On 4 May 1961, seven black and six white people decided to test two such cases: *Morgan v. Virginia* (1946) and *Boynton v. Virginia* (1960). The activists hoped their riding on interstate buses and using bus facilities reserved for the opposite race would induce a backlash from racist southerners. This, in turn, it was thought, would force the US government to see to it that the Constitution was followed.

First Freedom Ride

James Farmer, one of the founders of the Congress of Racial Equality (CORE) in 1941, organized what was to be known as the Freedom Rides. He and several CORE and SNCC members planned to ride on two buses from Washington, DC to New Orleans, Louisiana. On the buses, and at each stop, they planned to break the segregation norms of separation. Their journey and the ones it inspired would finally bring an end to the segregated buses and bus terminal facilities, but not without serious injury to many of the participants.

Timeline of the Freedom Rides

- 4 May 1961: thirteen Freedom Riders set out on two buses.
- 14 May: outside Anniston, Alabama, the first bus was stopped by a mob of 200. The bus was set on fire. The passengers escaped from the bus only to be set on by the angry white people. They were beaten and almost lynched before highway patrolmen fired shots into the air. The white Freedom Riders were singled out for worse beatings for being 'nigger lovers'.
- 14 May: when the second bus arrived in Anniston, local Ku Klux Klan members boarded the bus and beat up the Freedom Riders. The bus continued to Birmingham where the Freedom Riders were attacked with baseball bats, iron pipes and chains. The Riders decided to fly to New Orleans after serious threats were made and after bus drivers refused to drive the buses.
- 17 May: a new group of Freedom Riders led by a college student, Diane Nash, set out from Nashville. On arrival in Birmingham, they were promptly arrested.
- 20 May: the Freedom Ride continued from Birmingham to Montgomery. The Riders were escorted by police until they reached the city limits of Montgomery. Once they arrived at the bus terminal, a white mob beat them. The police did not intervene. Ambulances refused to take the injured to the hospital. Local blacks saved the Freedom Riders.
- 21 May: 1500 people packed into the First Baptist Church in Montgomery. Several important civil rights speakers addressed the crowd, including Ralph Abernathy, Martin Luther King, Jr and James Farmer. A mob of over 3000 white people gathered outside the church. After a telephone plea from King to Robert Kennedy Jr, the US **attorney general**, US marshals dispersed the crowd with tear gas.
- 22 May: More CORE and SNCC Freedom Riders arrived in Montgomery. The Kennedy administration had secretly arranged with the governors of Alabama and Mississippi to provide protection to the Riders. In exchange, local police would be allowed to arrest Freedom Riders when they tried to use whites-only facilities.
- June–September: Attorney General Kennedy asked for a 'cooling off' period but the Freedom Riders refused. More than 60 Freedom Rides took place throughout the South. The Riders usually converged on Jackson, Mississippi. There, hundreds were arrested.
- 1 November: new regulations went into effect that compelled the Interstate Commerce Commission to desegregate buses and bus terminals.

ANALYSING A HISTORIAN'S ARGUMENTS

In the following source, Dr Arsenault analyses how several groups responded to the Freedom Riders. Answer the questions after Source F in order to examine the evidence the historian uses to support his argument.

SOURCE F

Extract from Raymond Arsenault, *Freedom Riders: 1961 and the Struggle for Racial Justice*, Oxford University Press, Oxford, 2006, pages 345–6. Arsenault is an American historian specializing in the history of the South.

In Mississippi, the task of uncovering the criminal backgrounds of the Freedom Riders had already been delegated to the State Sovereignty Commission, an investigative and propaganda agency established in 1956. Working in close cooperation with the highway patrol and the White Citizens' Councils, the commission was empowered 'to do and perform any and all acts and things deemed necessary and proper to protect the sovereignty of the State of Mississippi, and her sister states'. … the Sovereignty Commission patterned itself after the FBI, targeting alleged subversives and troublemakers. Even before the first group of Freedom Riders arrived in Mississippi, the commission was on the case, compiling information on CORE, SNCC, and movement leaders. Once the rounds of arrests began, investigators monitored every aspect of the Freedom Rides, amassing files on each Rider

and scrutinizing anyone who publicly supported the Rides.

Although the stated rationale for this massive effort was the preservation of civic order, the driving force behind the Sovereignty Commission's investigative activities was the deeply held conviction that the civil rights movement, including the Freedom Rides, was connected to an international Communist conspiracy. The sense of panic that spread across much of the Deep South in the summer of 1961 was, first and foremost, a reaction to what appeared to be an impending loss of racial privilege and social control. But the intensity of the resistance to the Freedom Riders had a lot to do with the widespread perception that they were 'outside agitators' in the truest sense of the term, that they represented forces alien and hostile to American values. The notion that the Freedom Rides were part of a Communist plot first emerged in Alabama in mid-May when Bull Connor, Attorney General MacDonald Gallion, and others played upon Cold War suspicions of a grand conspiracy to subvert the Southern way of life.

5   What role did the Sovereignty Commission play in investigating the Freedom Riders?
6   According to the Sovereignty Commission, why were the Freedom Riders suspect?

VALUE AND LIMITATIONS OF EYEWITNESS ACCOUNTS

As you read Source G, consider the possible values and limitations of his statement:

• How many of each can you come up with?

• How can we confirm or refute what he said?

SOURCE G

Statement made by Albert Bigelow, a white member of CORE in his fifties. Bigelow made the statement on 25 May 1962 to a New York Committee of Inquiry (www.crmvet. org/riders/6205_core_coi_bigelow.pdf).

The first major violence against Freedom Riders occurred at Anniston, Ala., May 13, 1961. Bigelow on the police role there:

A crowd of 150, perhaps only 50 active, was ready for us at the Anniston station. Outside, no police were in sight. During fifteen minutes in Anniston, while the mob slashed tires and smashed windows, one policeman appeared in a brown uniform. He did nothing to stop vandalism but fraternized with the mob. A man in a white coverall with dark oval insignia on the breast was friendly with the policeman and consulted from time to time with the most active of the mob. Two police appeared and cleared a path. The bus left the station. There were no arrests.

A few miles out on the highway to Birmingham a tire blew and we pulled to the roadside, the mob after us in about

50 cars. They surrounded us again, yelling and smashing windows, brandishing clubs, chains and pipes; I saw all three. They surged around the bus, screamed obscenities and tried to board but were prevented by Eli Cowling of the State Highway police, in plainclothes, who, with a pistol, held back the mob from inside our door. We had thought Cowling an ordinary passenger. His single-handed action showed that a mob can be held off. Again Mr. Cowling stood in our door. For 15 or 20 minutes no other police were in sight. The bus was now being attacked with fury.

The man in the white coverall stood in front of the bus. A state trooper arrived, consulted the man in the coverall but did nothing to stop the vandalism.

After about 21 minutes at the roadside there was a very loud crash and shouts of 'sieg heil'. The bus, on fire now, filled with acrid, dense black smoke. All of us, fourteen I think, got out some jumping from windows. Across the highway, in a state patrol car, three or four police sat joking and laughing.

Non-violent protests: the Albany Movement (1961–2)

■ Efforts to totally desegregate a city

Because Albany, Georgia resisted any desegregation, SNCC and NAACP activists chose to focus their efforts there. The town had about 57,000 residents, half of whom were African American. In 1961, SNCC activists led by Charles Sherrod helped organize a series of protests. Hundreds were soon arrested for trying to desegregate transportation facilities as well as hotels and restaurants. The resisters invited Martin Luther King, Jr, hoping his presence would bring attention to the civil rights struggle. Various black organizations came together under an umbrella group known as the Albany Movement. The campaign was the first attempt to desegregate a whole city.

■ Police chief's strategy to defeat the desegregation campaign

The local police chief, Laurie Pritchett, came up with a strategy to outfox the protesters. Chief among his tactics were:

- Avoid violence at all costs. He knew this would bring federal and media attention to the protesters.
- Arrest large numbers of activists. Make sure there was plenty of jail space in Albany and other nearby towns. Eventually, the movement ran out of marchers willing to go to jail.
- When King and Abernathy were arrested, Pritchett made sure they were released from jail quickly so they would not become rallying points.
- After the federal government pressured the two sides to negotiate, the city agreed to desegregate. King left Albany and the protest ended. However, the city did not keep their side of the bargain and desegregation continued.

■ The failures of the Albany Movement

The Albany Movement was seen by some within the movement as a failure because:

- The campaign had not been planned properly. Some argued that by trying to desegregate many aspects of life in Albany at the same time, there was a lack of focus.
- There were clear divisions among the different civil rights groups. The NAACP, SCLC and SNCC were at odds on strategy. SNCC workers felt that King had taken over what had been organized as a community movement.
- The SCLC recognized that it would have to have deeper ties to the local community in order to organize more effectively.
- Kennedy's government did not intervene. Because of the lack of visible police violence, Kennedy did not feel pressured to act.

King felt he had learned important lessons on how better to organize, among them the need to develop the groundwork locally for subsequent actions. He also planned to focus on specific targets one at a time instead of a broad attack on many fronts.

■ New interpretations on the Albany Movement

In recent years, historians have altered their analysis of the aftermath of what had occurred in Albany. Many no longer regard the movement as a failure. Within a year, the city was largely desegregated and registration drives had successfully increased the African American electorate.

LACK OF HINDSIGHT

- When one is close to an event, it is sometimes difficult to see the bigger picture.

Read the following source and answer the questions that follow.

SOURCE H

Extract from Reese Cleghorn, 'Epilogue in Albany: Were the Mass Marches Worthwhile?', *The New Republic*, 30 July 1963. Quoted in Clayborne Carson, ed. *Reporting Civil Rights Part One: American Journalism 1941–1963*, Library of America, New York, 2003, pages 882–3. Cleghorn reported on the Civil Rights Movement for the *Atlanta Journal* and national publications.

Once the goal was to fill the jails. But the Albany City jail, which had working agreements with fortresses in neighboring counties, proved a bottomless pit. Not since Albany has anyone taken Dr. King literally when he has talked of filling the jails of the South …

Albany remains a monument to white supremacy. At this moment it represents at once the triumph of sophisticated segregation and the low point for the mass demonstration in this, the decade of the mass demonstration. It was here that the ambitious 'jail-ins' began, and here that they were found wanting. Does the outcome suggest what may happen in other urban centers of the old Southern plantation country, where segregation is only beginning to be tested? Police chief Laurie Pritchett, whose national acclaim has taken him to the podium of a Ford Foundation-sponsored seminar to tell other police chiefs how to handle racial protests, says about 30 police departments in the South have sent officers to learn from Albany.

7   According to Cleghorn, were the Albany marches successful?
8   How might a historian have interpreted the same events differently from Cleghorn? Why?

USING PHOTOGRAPHS AS HISTORICAL EVIDENCE

Look at the following source and answer the question which follows.

SOURCE I

Albany Police Chief Laurie Pritchett (right) speaks to civil rights leaders Reverend Martin Luther King, Jr and Dr William G. Anderson (centre) during an anti-segregation demonstration in Albany, Georgia, July 1962.

9   How can this photograph be used as evidence for a historian writing about the Albany Movement?

Freedom Summer (1964)

Revised ▢

■ Mississippi Summer Project

By the summer of 1964, SNCC leader Bob Moses decided that the federal government was moving far too slowly for any significant change to occur. He issued a call for hundreds of northern university students to come to Mississippi that summer to teach in schools and help black people register to vote, in what was known as the Mississippi Summer Project:

- Many of the more than 1000 out-of-state volunteers were white students.
- Before heading to Mississippi, they received a week of training in Oxford, Ohio.
- Their training included sessions on how to teach literacy and civics classes, register black people to vote, and promote an alternative Democratic party to the all-white Mississippi one.
- The volunteers were told they were embarking on a difficult and possibly dangerous activity in a very hostile environment.

■ The segregationist response

To many of the white Mississippians, the volunteers represented an invading army from the North. The 6000-strong and growing White Knights of the Ku Klux Klan responded by burning black churches and beating civil rights workers. Local police authorities, in many cases, aided these violent activities.

■ 'Mississippi Burning'

On the afternoon of 21 June 1964, two young CORE activists and one recently arrived northern student volunteer were arrested by the police for speeding in Philadelphia, Mississippi. The local Klan chapter was informed of this, and when the three were released from jail, their car was followed. They were never seen alive again. In response to a national outcry over the missing men, President Lyndon Johnson ordered the Federal Bureau of Investigation (FBI) to investigate the disappearances. The operation was codenamed 'Mississippi Burning'. It took six weeks to locate the remains of the men. Nineteen white people were implicated in the murders, but the state refused to prosecute. It was only in 1967 that seven people involved in the case were convicted on lesser charges. This marked the first time a Mississippi jury had convicted Klansmen in connection with the death of a black man.

■ Results of Freedom Summer

- During the course of the summer, more than 40 Freedom schools were set up and 3000 young people learned community organizing and black history.
- However, of the 17,000 African Americans who attempted to register, only 1600 applications were accepted by the local authorities.
- Murders, beatings and church burnings continued through the summer.
- Divisions began to appear among civil rights workers.
- There was some resentment felt by local SNCC and CORE workers who knew they had to live the segregationist nightmare every day instead of just one single summer while outsiders would leave after several months.
- This divide was furthered as some jobs previously done by black people were taken by white people from outside Mississippi.
- There were also intense discussions about the value of a non-violent response in the face of continued white southern aggression.

SPOT THE INFERENCE

- Answers that score in the top mark bands avoid excessive summarizing or paraphrasing of the sources.
- They instead make inferences from the sources, as well as analysing their value in terms of their context.

Below is a source and a series of statements. Read the source and decide which of the statements:

- **make inference from the source [I]**

- **paraphrase the source [P]**

- **summarize the source [S]**

- **cannot be justified from the source [X].**

Statement	I	P	S	X
President Johnson ordered the FBI to arrest the murderers				
Moses thought public opinion could be changed by parents' action				
Without government intervention, violence would continue				
The government was slow to act in the Philadelphia, Mississippi case and delayed action for a day				

SOURCE J

Letter from Robert Moses to the parents of the Mississippi Summer Volunteers, June 1964 (www.crmvet.org/docs/64_msfs_parents_letter.pdf).

Immediate action is needed by all those concerned with the safety of the Mississippi Summer Volunteers. Unless the President and the Attorney General can be convinced of the need for Federal protection of civil rights workers in Mississippi, the events of Philadelphia are almost certain to be repeated over and over again in the next two months.

We are asking all parents to use their influence in the coming week to pressure President Johnson and Attorney General Kennedy into a commitment to protect workers before violence occurs, instead of waiting until the worst has happened before they offer their help. To help you understand what can be done, it is necessary to stress the following points.

The mood of Mississippi today is one of mounting tension. Acts of violence or near violence are increasing. We have enclosed a two-page report on incidents from one twenty-four period. The 16 incidents in the report show that violence is not limited to any section of the state and that intimidation takes an unlimited variety of forms.

The Federal Government did not act quickly enough in the Philadelphia case. We are enclosing a chronology of the attempts of COFO [Council of Federated Organizations] to obtain an FBI investigation or other Federal aid in the Philadelphia incident. This report shows that it took 24 hours – undoubtedly the critical 24 hours – to get the Federal Government to act. FBI agents in Mississippi are always white, generally Southern and usually from Mississippi itself. Like local law enforcement officers, these agents often serve to obstruct, rather than aid, the administration of justice in civil rights cases. The enclosed chronology deals only with Federal contacts; local police changed their story continually and were useless in the attempt to locate the missing persons.

The Civil Rights Act (1964)

Revised ☐

■ President Johnson's reasons for wanting a civil rights bill

President Johnson was determined to push through President Kennedy's civil rights legislation. Kennedy had proposed a bill that would end discrimination in public facilities. That said, Johnson had his own vision of what he called the Great Society. He hoped to put 'an end to poverty and racial injustice'. This was on a much larger scale than Kennedy's proposal.

Among the reasons he wanted to pass the Civil Rights Act were:

- He wanted to prove his liberal credentials as a southerner.
- He believed the bill would be a wonderful tribute to President Kennedy.
- He had taught poor Mexican Americans and knew first hand how damaging poverty, prejudice and poor schooling could be.
- He firmly believed that ending racial tension would increase economic opportunity and that the South would improve economically as a result.
- He had supported the Supreme Court's *Brown v. Board of Education* decision.
- He was one of the few southern politicians who had not signed the Southern Manifesto.

■ Congressional opposition to civil rights

President Kennedy's civil rights bill, or draft law, which he had introduced in June 1963 was delayed intentionally in Congress. Even though opinion polls showed most Americans approved of the president's plan, there was significant opposition in the Senate. Johnson used his considerable political skills to move his version of the bill forward. Although the bill passed easily in the House of Representatives, the Senate was more difficult. Southern senators held up a vote on the bill for months by using Senate rules to prevent a vote. Johnson bullied, cajoled and flattered his former colleagues in Congress to move forward on this important legislation. Johnson was well aware that the only way he could get his bill passed was to enlist the aid of the opposition Republicans because many southern Democrats were adamantly opposed to desegregation.

■ Johnson's appeals to the Republicans

Johnson felt that Everett Dirksen, the Republican leader in the Senate, was the key. Johnson hoped to make the bill a cross-party bill and not just a Democratic Party one. In order to accomplish this, the president enlisted Dirksen's aid and allowed him to make some minor changes to the legislation. Dirksen, in the end, was able to bring along most of his party colleagues.

Other groups also put continual pressure on members of Congress. These included the major African American groups such as the NAACP, SNCC and SCLC, as well as the powerful AFL-CIO (American Federation of Labor and Congress of Industrial Organizations).

■ Passage of the Civil Rights Act

On 2 July 1964, the Civil Rights Act was passed. All southern Democratic senators except for one voted against the bill. In the House of Representatives, 25% had voted against the measure. Many southern Democrats turned against their party and would vote for Republican candidates for decades after the vote. Lyndon Johnson signed the Act into law at the White House. Among the many important civil rights leaders and politicians in attendance were Martin Luther King, Jr, A. Philip Randolph, Roy Wilkins, James Forman, Dorothy Height, the Attorney General Robert Kennedy, Senator Hubert Humphrey and Senator Everett Dirksen. The ceremony and the president's speech were broadcast live to the nation.

RELEVANCE OF ORIGIN AND PURPOSE IN DETERMINING A HISTORIAN'S VIEWS

The following two secondary sources examine why President Johnson wanted to pass a significant civil rights bill. Read the two sources closely and read the description in bold before the text and then answer the questions that follow.

SOURCE K

Extract from Robert Dallek, *Lyndon B. Johnson: Portrait of a President*, Oxford University Press, Oxford, 2004, page 163. Dallek is an American historian specializing in US presidents.

He had several reasons for wanting to make good on civil rights. First, he felt that passing Kennedy's bill would help heal the wound opened by his assassination. To Johnson's thinking, the President's murder resulted from the violence and hatred dividing America and tearing at its social fabric. As important, there was the moral issue or the matter of fairness that Johnson felt with a keenness few could fully understand. Johnson, the most powerful political leader in the world, was also Johnson, the poor boy from Texas, who identified with and viscerally experienced the suffering of the disadvantaged.

He repeatedly told the story of Zephyr Wright, his cook, 'a college graduate', who, when driving the Vice President's official car with her husband from Washington to Texas, couldn't use the facilities in a gas station to relieve herself. 'When they had to go to the bathroom,' Johnson told Mississippi Senator John Stennis, 'they would … pull off on a side road, and Zephyr Wright, the cook of the Vice President of the United States, would squat in the road to pee.' He told Stennis: 'That's wrong. And there ought to be something to change that. And it seems to me that if people in Mississippi don't change it voluntarily, that it's just going to be necessary to change it by law.'

SOURCE L

Extract from David Goldfield, 'Border Men: Truman, Eisenhower, Johnson, and Civil Rights'. *Journal of Southern History*, February 2014, Vol. 80, Issue 1, pages 33–4. Goldfield is an American historian at the University of North Carolina.

When Johnson ascended to the presidency after the tragedy in Dallas, it was a liberation from the bonds of regionalism and from the politics of ambition. He was not Lyndon Johnson southerner or westerner; he was Lyndon Johnson, American. In his first speech after taking office, Johnson vowed to carry on the legacy of JFK in civil rights.

Considering Kennedy's meager record – a fine speech on the morality of racial equality and a bill ending segregation in public facilities submitted to Congress, but not acted upon – the reference was more rhetorical than real. Yet 50 percent of the country believed Kennedy had been moving too quickly on civil rights. So, as one Kennedy scholar has noted, 'The larger Kennedy strategy on civil rights was to pursue glacial change.'

That pace would not work for Johnson. He wanted a civil rights act, and he wanted it now. He wanted to secure his legacy as a modem-day Abraham Lincoln to show those Ivy Leaguers and northern liberals that he could accomplish what they had not. 'I'm going to be the President who finishes what Lincoln began,' he insisted. And, in the process, he would lift up the South to full participation in American life. 'Those civil righters are going to have to wear sneakers to keep up with me,' he vowed.

10 What can we determine from the origin and purpose of each source that would help explain his viewpoint and analysis?

11 Look closely at the origin of each source. What time period do the book and article cover? When were they published? Can we tell anything from the author's background?

■ Impact of the Civil Rights Act

■ The changes the Civil Rights Act brought

The Civil Rights Act of 1964 challenged some of the worst aspects of Jim Crow laws in the South. Among the changes provided by the Act were:

- Federal intervention to desegregate schools, swimming pools, parks and other public facilities.
- The establishment of the Equal Employment Opportunity Commission to investigate claims of racial and sexual discrimination for companies with at least 25 employees.
- Restricted the use of literacy tests when blacks tried to register to vote.
- Prohibited discrimination on the basis of race, colour, religion or national origin in hotels, restaurants and places of entertainment.
- Prohibited discrimination of those who received federal funds based on race, colour and national origin.

President Johnson used the power of the federal government to ensure that the new laws were enforced. For example, the government stopped providing funds to schools that failed to integrate. Schools that were desegregating received more funds. Johnson also increased the amount of funds poor black colleges received through his Higher Education Act of 1964. The number of black college students skyrocketed by 400% during the 1960s largely due to increased aid to these educational institutions.

■ Resistance to the Civil Rights Act

Nonetheless, resistance in much of the South continued. Schools were, by and large, segregated. Only 1.18% of black students attended schools with white students. Some businesses closed rather than allow black people in, while others transformed themselves into private clubs so they could evade the Civil Rights Act. Voter registration continued at a snail's pace in the Deep South and many rules and regulations prevented most African Americans from exercising their constitutional right to be put on the voter rolls.

■ The racial situation in the North

Outside the South, *de facto* discrimination existed in schooling and housing. African Americans in cities such as New York, Chicago, Detroit and Los Angeles were often forced to live in ghettos where they faced high unemployment and poor living conditions. Some civil rights leaders also began to question the strategy of working with the federal government and white liberals because of the slow pace of reforms. More demonstrations and protests would be needed for black people to finally be allowed to exercise their fundamental right to vote in the southern states.

Nonetheless, the Civil Rights Act was the most important legislation concerning race since Reconstruction, almost 100 years earlier. The federal government had finally taken a strong stand against the institutionalized system of racism, especially in the southern states. It marked the first serious step of several to create a more equal America.

ANALYSING A HISTORIAN'S VIEWPOINT

- You will most likely have at least one source in Paper 1 that is an extract from a historian's work.
- It is important when you read the source to determine the different ideas raised by the historian.

Read the following extract by the noted American historian James Patterson. Use the chart below to list what he thinks were the problems that were not solved by the 1964 Civil Rights Act and what were the positive outcomes of the legislation.

SOURCE M

Extract from James T. Patterson, *Grand Expectations: The United States, 1945–1974*, Oxford University Press, New York, 1996, pages 545–6. Patterson is a professor emeritus of American History at Brown University.

No law, of course can work wonders overnight, and the 1964 Civil Rights Act was no exception. Voting rights remained to be protected. Many employers and unions evaded the strictures against job discrimination. De facto racial discrimination remained widespread in the North, especially in housing and schooling. Many school districts, mainly in the Deep South, continued to employ ruses of one sort or another to avoid desegregation in public education … . Finally, the law did not pretend to do anything to better the mostly abysmal economic conditions of black people in the United States. Like the war on poverty, it was a liberal, not a radical, measure. It aimed to promote legal, not social, equality.

The Civil Rights Act was nonetheless a significant piece of legislation, far and away the most important in the history of American race relations. Quickly upheld by the Supreme Court, it was enforced with vigor by the Johnson administration. That required a huge expansion in the reach of the State, for there were many thousands of hospitals, school districts, and colleges and universities affected by the provisions of the law. Although many southern leaders resisted, most aspects of enforcement proved effective in time, and the seemingly impregnable barriers of Jim Crow finally began to fall. Black people at last could begin to enjoy equal access to thousands of places that had excluded them in the past. Few laws have had such dramatic and heart-warming effects.

Unsolved problems	Successes
•	•
•	•
•	•
•	•
•	•
•	•

Selma

Shortcomings of the Civil Rights Act

While important, the 1964 Civil Rights Act did not end segregation. It took time, energy and money to desegregate schools, buses, hotels, restaurants and parks. The vast majority of black Americans in the South still not have the right to vote. The states with the lowest number of registered black voters included Mississippi, Alabama and Georgia.

Obstacles to voting in Selma, Alabama

Selma in Dallas County, Alabama stood out as a glaring example of the difficulties African Americans had in voting. Among the obstacles that stood in their way were the following:

- The registration office was only open two Mondays, with irregular hours, each month.
- Applicants suffered long delays and had to answer lengthy questionnaires.
- The slightest error on a questionnaire meant disqualification.
- Registrars sometimes asked applicants if their employers knew they were trying to register to vote; applicants rightly feared for their jobs.

Unsurprisingly, only 383 of the 15,000 black people in Dallas County were registered to vote. It was in this climate that a local civil rights activist, Amelia Boynton, invited Martin Luther King, Jr to come to Selma. King viewed the situation in Selma as a good opportunity to focus national attention on the terrible plight of the black people in Dallas County. Selma also had a violent racist, Jim Clark, as sheriff and he could be used as a lightning rod to highlight the official violence directed at black people. King and other civil rights leaders hoped that a showdown in Selma would result in pushing the federal government to pass a voting rights act.

Mass arrests

In January 1965, King and SNCC leader John Lewis marched to Selma's courthouse where voter registration took place. At first, the marchers were left in peace but over the following days hundreds were arrested, including King, for gathering without a permit. King wrote a letter from jail and had it appear as an advertisement in the *New York Times*. King wrote that, 'Why are we in jail? Have you ever been required to answer 100 questions on government, some abstruse even to a political scientist specialist, merely to vote? Have you ever stood in line with over a hundred others and after waiting an entire day seen less than ten given the qualifying test?

'THIS IS SELMA, ALABAMA. THERE ARE MORE NEGROES IN JAIL WITH ME THAN THERE ARE ON THE VOTING ROLLS.'

Soon there were more than 3000 protesters in jail. A federal judge intervened and demanded that the registrar stop using complicated tests and that he enrol 100 people per day when the office was open.

Nonetheless, the atmosphere in Alabama was increasingly violent. After a black veteran, Jimmie Lee Jackson, was shot dead while trying to protect his mother from being beaten by police, civil rights leaders decided to march from Selma to Montgomery, the state capital.

USING A SOURCE AND YOUR OWN KNOWLEDGE

Read the preceding page and the source below and then answer the questions that follow.

SOURCE N

Extract from John Lewis, *Walking in the Wind: A Memoir of the Movement*, Simon & Schuster, New York, 1998, page 306. The civil rights activist was the chairman of SNCC in 1965. He was in Selma when King came to the town.

We in SNCC had known for a long time, and the SCLC learned quickly, that Clark's short fuse made him an easy target for provocation. And since he considered the county courthouse – where all voters were registered – his personal domain, it was inevitable that we would square off against him. That's what we prepared for … .

But the day that King first came to Selma to speak was calm. There was no march on the courthouse, not yet. There was no showdown with Jim Clark, not yet. This was a rally, a laying down of the gauntlet. Dr. King told the audience that if Governor Wallace and the Alabama state legislature didn't force Dallas County to begin registering its black citizens, 'We will seek to arouse the federal government by marching by the thousands.' He even threatened another March on Washington. 'We must be willing to go to jail,' he said, again, 'by the thousands.'

12 How do they complement each other?

13 How can we use the two to answer the following question: what does Source N and the text tell us about the civil rights strategy at Selma?

INTERPRETING A PHOTO

Look at the photo caption and the photo below. Answer the question which follows.

SOURCE O

Two Mississippi Summer Project volunteers helping a couple register to vote.

14 Why do you think the couple needed assistance in filling out the voter registration form?

Bloody Sunday (7 March 1965)

Revised

■ Bloody Sunday

SNCC and SCLC led the march of 600 local residents on 7 March. The two groups hoped to show a united front to strengthen their case for a voting rights act. John Lewis, SNCC leader, and Hosea Williams, a top King aide, were at the front of the marchers. As they approached the Edmund Pettis Bridge, they were met by Alabama state troopers. The troopers set on the marchers and beat, whipped and gassed them on what became known as Bloody Sunday. The horrific violence was filmed by TV news stations and shown nationwide. The reaction was immediate. Americans were disgusted what they saw on television, especially given the peaceful nature of the marchers. Protest demonstrations took place in cities across America and more than 100 senators and congressmen called for voting rights.

■ Ministers' march

On 9 March, King called for a 'ministers' march':

- He encouraged religious leaders from all denominations to join him.
- Over 1500 black and white demonstrators set off.
- They were stopped at the same bridge where the violent demonstrations had taken place two days earlier and told to disperse.
- The marchers prayed together and then turned around.
- SNCC leaders were upset by what they viewed as King's cowardice, not knowing that King had secretly made an agreement with the federal government to do this.
- Alabama governor George Wallace had banned the march.
- His decision was upheld by a federal judge.
- That same night, three white ministers were attacked by segregationists and one, James Reeb, died of his injuries.

■ Selma to Montgomery march

The murder sparked more outrage across the USA. President Johnson spoke to both houses of Congress on 15 March, pleading with them to write a voting rights bill. He also expressed solidarity with the marchers by ending his speech with the civil rights slogan, 'We shall overcome'. King responded to the speech by stating that, 'Never has a President spoken so eloquently or so sincerely on the question of civil rights.' A new march was planned and, when the governor again declared it illegal, a federal judge overruled him. On 21 March, 3200 marchers set out on the 54-mile (87-km) route to the state capital. This time, though, the federal government provided protection in the form of 2000 troops, helicopters and planes. Among the notable civil rights leaders were King, Lewis, Ralph Abernathy and Roy Wilkins. Jewish, Catholic and Protestant religious leaders also joined in, as did Ralph Bunche, the UN Under-Secretary for Special Political Affairs.

Four days later, the marchers arrived in Montgomery. King addressed a crowd of 25,000. He urged the passing of legislation to permit blacks to vote. Governor Wallace refused to accept a petition from the marchers.

VALUE AND LIMITATIONS OF PUBLIC SPEECHES

● A speech can provide us with important insights into an event or the viewpoint of the one delivering the speech.

Read Source P and try to come up with at least two values and two limitations of the speech for a historian studying what occurred at Selma in 1965.

SOURCE P

Dr King speaking before 25,000 people in Montgomery, Alabama at the end of the march on 25 March 1965 (https://kinginstitute.stanford.edu/our-god-marching).

My dear and abiding friends, Ralph Abernathy, and to all of the distinguished Americans seated here on the rostrum, my friends and co-workers of the state of Alabama, and to all of the freedom-loving people who have assembled here this afternoon from all over our nation and from all over the world: Last Sunday, more than eight thousand of us started on a mighty walk from Selma, Alabama. We have walked through desolate valleys and across the trying hills. We have walked on meandering highways and rested our bodies on rocky byways. Some of our faces are burned from the outpourings of the sweltering sun. Some have literally slept in the mud. We have been drenched by the rains.

But today as I stand before you and think back over that great march, I can say, as Sister Pollard said – a seventy-year-old Negro woman who lived in this community during the bus boycott – and one day, she was asked while walking if she didn't want to ride. And when she answered, 'No', the person said, 'Well, aren't you tired?' And with her ungrammatical profundity, she said, 'My feets is tired, but my soul is rested.' (Yes, sir. All right) And in a real sense this afternoon, we can say that our feet are tired, (Yes, sir) but our souls are rested.

Values	Limitations
1	1
2	2

Voting Rights Act of 1965

■ Johnson's speech to Congress, 15 March 1965

A week after Bloody Sunday, President Johnson addressed both houses of Congress. He delivered an impassioned speech in which he said that, 'There is no Negro problem. There is no Southern problem. There is no Northern problem. There is only an American problem … we are met here as Americans to solve that problem.' The President continued, 'There is no constitutional issue here. The command of the Constitution is plain. There is no moral issue. It is wrong – deadly wrong – to deny your fellow Americans the right to vote in this country. There is no issue of states' rights or national rights. There is only the struggle for human rights. …' Members of Congress, with the exception of the segregationists, jumped to their feet and applauded Johnson, when he ended his speech with the anthem of the Civil Rights Movement, 'We – shall – overcome!' Martin Luther King, Jr watched the speech on television in Montgomery, Alabama, and wept.

■ Legislative negotiations

A bill was introduced on 17 March, jointly sponsored by the Senate Majority leader, Mike Mansfield, and the Senate Minority leader, Everett Dirksen. The attorney general, Nicholas Katzenbach, had helped to write the bill. President Johnson knew he needed Republican support because he was afraid that the southern Democrats might **filibuster** the bill. After over two months of debate and negotiations, the bill passed on 26 May. On 9 July, the House of Representatives passed its version.

A conference committee was then appointed in order to resolve the differences between the two versions. There were serious disagreements over whether or not poll taxes should be outlawed completely. This last hurdle was overcome when Dr King gave his approval to a compromise in which the Justice Department would sue states that kept poll taxes. Northern liberals now felt they could support the bill wholeheartedly. Both houses signed the new bill by 4 August.

On 6 August 1965, President Johnson signed the Voting Rights Act into law. In addition to the many US politicians in attendance were Wilkins, Farmer, Lewis and King, the leaders of the four major civil rights groups, as well as Rosa Parks.

Among the results of the Civil Rights Act of 1965 were:

- The 15th Amendment was enforced.
- All US citizens aged 21 years and older were allowed to vote.
- Literacy and other tests for registration were made illegal.
- The number of black voters increased from 35% to 65% in the four years following the Act.
- Many more blacks were elected to political office.
- Overt racism began to fade slowly in the South.

2 Protests and action

SYNTHESIZING INFORMATION

- One key to success in Paper 1 is the ability to take information from a source and from your own knowledge and create your own analysis.

Read the following source closely and the preceding page. Then, try to answer the questions using the source and the information from the text.

SOURCE Q

Extract from *Black Power: The Politics of Liberation in America*, 1967, by SNCC activist Stokely Carmichael and the political scientist Charles Hamilton. Quoted in Clayborne Carson, ed., *The Eyes on the Prize Civil Rights Reader*, Penguin Books, New York, 1991, pages 265–6.

From March to August, 1965, about fifty to sixty black citizens made their way to the courthouse to register and successfully passed the registration 'test'. Then, in August, the 1965 Voting Right Act was passed and federal 'examiners' or registrars came into the county. No longer did a black man face literacy tests or absurdly difficult questions about the Constitution or such tactics as rejecting because one 't' was not properly crossed or an 'i' inadequately dotted. The voting rolls swelled by the hundreds … .

The *act* of registering to vote does several things. It marks the beginning of political modernization by broadening the base of participation. It also does something the existentialists talk about: it gives one a sense of being. The black man who goes to register is saying to the white man, 'No'. His is saying: 'You have said that I cannot vote. You have said that this is my place. This where I should remain. You have contained me and I am saying "No" to your containment. I am stepping out of bounds. I am saying "No" to you and thereby I am creating a better life for myself. I am resisting someone who has contained me.' That is what the first act does. The black person begins to live. He begins to create his *own* existence when he says 'no' to someone who contains him.

15 Why was registering to vote so important to African Americans?
16 What were the results of the 1965 Voting Rights Act?

SECTION 2 **Exam focus**

Source booklet

Read Source A below and answer question 14 in the accompanying question paper.

SOURCE A

Immediately after Rosa Parks had been arrested on 1 December 1955 for violating Montgomery, Alabama's bus segregation law, the Women's Political Council secretly issued a mimeographed (low-cost duplication) leaflet that called for a one-day boycott of the city buses (www.crmvet.org/docs/mbbleaf.htm).

This is for Monday, December 5, 1955

Another Negro woman has been arrested and thrown in jail because she refused to get up out of her seat on the bus for a white person to sit down.

It is the second time since the Claudette Colbert case that a Negro women has been arrested for the same thing. This has to be stopped.

Negroes have rights, too, for if Negroes did not ride the buses, they could not operate. Three-fourths of the riders are Negroes, yet we are arrested, or have to stand over empty seats. If we do not do something to stop these arrests, they will continue. The next time it may be you, or your daughter, or mother.

This woman's case will come up on Monday. We are, therefore, asking every Negro to stay off the busses Monday in protest of the arrest and trial. Don't ride the busses to work, to town, to school, or anywhere on Monday.

You can afford to stay out of school for one day if you have no other way to go except by bus.

You can also afford to stay out of town for one day. If you work, take a cab, or walk. But please, children and grown-ups, don't ride the bus at all on Monday. Please stay off of all buses Monday.

Sample question and answer

Below is a sample answer. Read it and the comments around it.

- Question 14 of Paper 1 requires students to evaluate the value and limitations of a source based on its origin, purpose and content.
- The question is worth 4 marks. The best way to ensure the demands of the question are fully addressed is to use the terms origin, purpose, content, value and limitation in the response.
- Using these terms makes it easier to ensure a response has fully addressed the question and makes it easier for an examiner to identify that all demands of the question have been addressed.
- You will notice that the question is asking you to analyse the value and limitations of a source for historians studying a particular event or action in history.
- Be sure to keep this in mind when answering the question
- You should address question 14 in a paragraph.
- You should spend about ten minutes answering this question.

14 With reference to its origin, purpose and content, evaluate the value and limitations of Source A, below, for a historian studying the Montgomery Bus Boycott.

Source A <u>originates</u> from a secretly produced leaflet created in 1955 by the Women's Political Council in Montgomery, Alabama. The <u>origin</u> has <u>value</u> because it is the first response to Rosa Parks' arrest. The <u>purpose</u> of the leaflet was to urge the citizens of Montgomery to stage a one-day boycott of the city buses because Rosa Parks had been arrested for refusing to surrender her seat to a white customer. The source has <u>value</u> for historians because its purpose clearly indicates the quick response of the women's group. It is also <u>valuable</u> because the <u>content</u> clearly states what the problem was and how best to demonstrate the community's outrage over Rosa Parks' arrest. The source is <u>limited</u> in several respects. Because the leaflet was published so soon after Parks' arrest, the historian does not know from the <u>content</u> whether or not people did stay at home or walk or take taxis to work. The <u>origin</u> may also be limited because it is unclear what the Women's Political Council was and how much support it had in the community.

This is a good start, because the response immediately begins to address the demands of the question starting with origin, which is made clear with the underlining.

The response wastes no words and immediately proceeds in the next sentence to address the purpose of the source, again underlining the word 'purpose' for emphasis.

The limitations of the origin and content are clearly stated.

4/4. This response gets full marks because it addresses every demand of the question: origin, purpose, content, value and limitation. These are easy to identify because those terms were used and underlined in the response. This makes it easy for the examiner to identify them and for the student to guarantee they have all been used in the response. Every sentence addresses origin, purpose, content, value and/or content, making it a highly focused response. Most importantly, the value and limitations are explained and connected to origin, purpose and/or content.

Exam practice

Now it's your turn to take a mock exam.

Read Sources M–P and answer questions 13–16 in the accompanying question paper. The sources and questions relate to Case study 1: The Civil Rights Movement in the United States 1954–65 – protests and action.

SOURCE M

Oral history interview with Andrew Young, 31 January 1974, Southern Oral History Program Collection, University of North Carolina, Chapel Hill. Young was an early civil rights leader and close associate of Martin Luther King, Jr.

See, the north [*sic*] was separated geographically, while the South was separated legally. Now, once the legal barriers in the South came down, people were fairly comfortable together. It was amazing to me to see that happen. And we were in Saint Augustine [Florida] when Lyndon Johnson signed the Civil Rights Act. And the very same hotel where our waitresses poured hot coffee on us, and where the manager poured acid on people trying to get in his swimming pool, and, I mean, just extremely violent reactions … the second of July Lyndon Johnson signed the Civil Rights Act of 1964. The fifth of July we went back to that same restaurant, and those people were just wonderful. I mean, they were apologetic. They said, 'We were just afraid of losing our businesses. We didn't want to be the only ones to be integrated. But if everybody's got to do it, we've been ready for it a long time ago. We're so glad the president signed this law and now we can be through with these troubles.' And so you didn't have that possibility of immediate change in the north, because people are geographically separated; they don't know each other. You don't have the stable leadership patterns in the north. I mean you had three generations of Ivan Allens in Atlanta, and three generations of Martin Luther Kings that have known each other. And Ivan Allen, Jr, who is the ex-mayor, is a friend of Martin Luther King, Sr. But Martin's grandfather was a Baptist preacher who was a good friend of the first Ivan Allen. And there are stable family ties. There's a stable leadership structure in the South, that moves things very rapidly, once people make up their minds. You don't have three generations of black leadership in any northern city.

SOURCE N

President Johnson signing the Civil Rights Act of 1964.

SOURCE O

Extract from Nick Kotz, *Judgment Days: Lyndon Baines Johnson, Martin Luther King, Jr., and the Laws that Changed America*, Houghton Mifflin Harcourt, New York, 2006, page 133. Kotz is an American journalist and historian.

Lyndon Johnson was now practicing what he had earlier preached to Jack Kennedy – taking the moral issue of civil rights directly to the South. Southerners may not like what you say, Johnson had advised Kennedy, but they will respect you for stating where you stand. Johnson left no doubt where he stood. In a speech at a Democratic Party dinner in Miami on February 27, the president had pledged to 'press forward with legislation and with education – and, yes, with action – until we have eliminated the last barrier of intolerance.' Speaking before the Georgia state legislature on May 8, Johnson told lawmakers 'not to heed those who would come waving the tattered and discredited banners of the past, who seek to stir old hostilities and kindle old hatreds, who preach battle between neighbors and bitterness between states'. The president summoned a vision of a new South that would cast off its legacy of poverty and racism and join 'the entire nation to ensure that every man enjoys all the rights secured him by the American Constitution'. The Georgia legislators gave the president a standing ovation.

Even in [Senator] Richard Russell's segregated Georgia, the assertion of moral leadership by the president and by church leaders seemed to move public opinion. In early 1964 the Georgia state senate surprisingly ratified the constitutional amendment outlawing the poll tax that long had been used to keep poor blacks from voting. Russell described the Georgia vote as personally 'humiliating'.

SOURCE P

Extract from leading Republican presidential candidate Barry Goldwater in a New York City fund-raising event on 12 May 1964. Goldwater would run and lose against President Johnson that year.

Now, Republicans want to see government, as our declaration says, helping the cause of equal opportunity. They don't want to see government as a cheerleader for a frightful game of violence, destruction and disobedience. And, once again, I point to the Republican principle of getting things done at the local level before calling out the Federal programs or the Federal troops.

Now, where are the states which today are witnessing the most violence? And I sadly remind you that they are the very states where there is the most talk about brotherhood and the very least opportunity for achieving it.

And I sadly remind you tonight that we are seeing violence in those very states which are proving that new laws alone are not the answer. There are too many of the old laws which aren't even working.

And then there is this above all, the oldest law of all: You can't pass a law that will make me like you or you like me. Let me remind my audience tonight that this is something that can only happen in our hearts. This is a problem of the heart and the mind, not the problem of the lawyer, the problem of the Senator, the Congressman or the President. This is a problem that is as old as the world …

The right to vote, of course. The right to seek an education, of course. There are laws, good laws, to secure these rights. But until we have an Administration that will cool the fires and the tempers of violence, we simply cannot solve the rest.

13 a What, according to Source P, were the failures of Johnson's government? [3]
 b What is suggested in Source N about the signing ceremony? [2]

14 With reference to its origin, purpose and content, analyse the value and limitations of Source O for a historian studying President Johnson's role in promoting civil rights. [4]

15 Compare and contrast how Sources M and O depict racial divisions in the South. [6]

16 Using the sources and your own knowledge, examine the political and social background to the passing of the 1964 Civil Rights Act. [9]

3 The role and significance of key actors/groups

Martin Luther King, Jr (1929–68)

▣ Importance of Martin Luther King, Jr

Of the many well-known civil rights activists, none was as recognizable as Martin Luther King, Jr. His oratory, passion, organizational skills, non-violent approach and ability to compromise made him one of the key actors in the racial drama of the 1950s and 1960s. His contributions helped lead to some of the most significant changes in civil rights equality in US history.

■ King's early life

King was born in 1929 in Atlanta, Georgia. He followed in his father's footsteps and became a Baptist minister. He earned a PhD in theology at Boston University. There, he began to be influenced by the non-violent civil disobedience philosophy of the Indian civil rights leader, Mohandas K. Gandhi. Other thinkers also helped him develop his ideology, much of which was based on Christian teachings.

■ King and the Montgomery Bus Boycott

In 1954, King became the pastor of Dexter Avenue Baptist Church in Montgomery, Alabama, at the age of 26. As the Montgomery Bus Boycott got underway, King was asked to head the Montgomery Improvement Association, a group created to help co-ordinate the efforts of the boycotters. King delivered his first speech on civil rights to hundreds of Montgomery residents attending a mass meeting. The success of the long boycott in desegregating the local bus system in 1956 brought attention to the young minister. From this point on, King was an instrumental force for social change.

■ King as head of the SCLC

In 1957, the newly formed Southern Christian Leadership Conference (SCLC) chose King as its president. The SCLC included several civil rights groups under its wing and King tried hard to keep the organization unified. This was not always possible given the very different strategies undertaken by different groups.

▣ Major civil rights events in King's life

Other important milestones in King's life included:

- The 1963 Birmingham Confrontation Campaign. The plan was to desegregate businesses and to boycott city stores. King was incarcerated and from jail he wrote his famous 'Letter from a Birmingham Jail'.
- In the same year, King participated in the March on Washington for Jobs and Freedom. It was in front of the Lincoln Memorial that King delivered his electrifying 'I Have a Dream' speech. The march and his speech helped push the Civil Rights Act forward.
- King campaigned in St Augustine, Florida.
- In 1964, King was awarded the Nobel Prize for Peace.
- The Selma to Montgomery March that King helped organize was one key to the passage of the significant Voting Rights Act of 1965.
- From 1965 to 1968, King focused on economic justice throughout the nation, and not solely on the South.

■ Opposition to Dr King

Part of Martin Luther King, Jr's strategy was to engage white people and enlist their aid in overturning Jim Crow laws. He also negotiated with the Kennedy and Johnson administrations and tried, not always successfully, to push the government to act forcefully in promoting equality. The director of the Federal Bureau of Investigation (FBI), J. Edgar Hoover, put King under surveillance beginning in 1955. Hoover hated King and felt he had been influenced by communists. There were also some civil rights activists who did not agree with the overall goal of social and economic integration with white America, while others felt that compromise only weakened the message and justice of the cause. Still others thought non-violence was not the best response to bombings, murders and beatings at the hands of the Ku Klux Klan (KKK) and police forces.

King was murdered by a white extremist in Memphis, Tennessee on 4 April 1968.

EXAMINING A SOURCE'S PURPOSE

- Question 14 of Paper 1 requires students to evaluate the value and limitations of a source based on its origin, purpose and content.
- The purpose of a source refers to why the author created the source. Knowing why a source was created can provide some insight into what kind of information was included and what kind of information may have been omitted.
- It also may give an indication to the perspective of the author. Answer the questions that follow Source A.

Below is the description of a source, Source A, that refers to the just and unjust laws.

SOURCE A

Extract from Martin Luther King, Jr's 'Letter from Birmingham City Jail.' King wrote this letter to a group of white ministers who had publicly criticized the tactics and rationale of Project Confrontation. It was first published by the American Friends Service Committee in May 1963 (http://teachingamericanhistory.org/library/document/letter-from-birmingham-city-jail/).

You express a great deal of anxiety over our willingness to break laws. This is certainly a legitimate concern. Since we so diligently urge people to obey the Supreme Court's decision of 1954 outlawing segregation in the public school, it is rather strange and paradoxical to find us consciously breaking laws. One may well ask, 'How can you advocate breaking some laws and obeying others?' The answer is found in the fact that there are two types of laws: there are *just* and there are *unjust* laws. I would be the first to advocate obeying just laws. One has not only a legal but moral responsibility to obey just laws. Conversely, one has a moral responsibility to disobey unjust laws. I would agree with Saint Augustine that 'An unjust law is not law at all.'

… Any law that uplifts human personality is just. Any law that degrades human personality is unjust. All segregation statutes are unjust because segregation distorts the soul and damages the personality. It gives the segregator a false sense of superiority and the segregated a false sense of inferiority … .

An unjust law is a code inflicted upon a minority which that minority had no part in enacting or creating because they did not have the unhampered right to vote. Who can say the legislature which set up the segregation laws was democratically elected? Throughout the state of Alabama all types of conniving methods are used to prevent Negroes from becoming registered voters and there are some counties without a single Negro registered to vote despite the fact that the Negro constitutes a majority of the population. Can any law set up in such a state be considered democratically structured?

1 Was this letter a public or private correspondence?
2 How would that change the purpose of the letter?
3 What specific points does Dr King raise in answer to the ones made by the white ministers?

Malcolm X (1925–65)

Revised ▢

■ Differences between Malcolm X and other civil rights leaders

Malcolm X represented a very different kind of black leader from those found in the ranks of the National Association for the Advancement of Colored People (NAACP) and the SCLC. His black nationalism stood in contrast to the integrationist impulses of people like Martin Luther King, Jr, Roy Wilkins or Thurgood Marshall. He was a mesmerizing speaker, a devout Muslim, and was mostly self-taught. He also had had a very difficult childhood and experienced racial hatred from an early age which coloured his views of white people.

■ Malcolm X's early life

Malcolm X was born as Malcolm Little in Omaha, Nebraska in 1925. His family was harassed by the KKK for anti-segregationist activity. His house was burned down and his father murdered. Soon, his mother was committed to a mental institution. Little finished eighth grade, the end of his formal schooling, and moved to Boston to live with his sister. Soon he became a petty thief and was convicted of burglary in 1946. He spent the next seven years in prison. It was there that he was first exposed to the black Muslim organization, the Nation of Islam (NOI). Malcolm Little found the teachings of the NOI appealing and soon converted. Black self-reliance and a strict moral code were at the heart of the NOI and Malcolm Little soon changed his name to Malcolm X. The X was meant to replace the 'slave name' Little.

■ Malcolm X and the NOI

Once out of prison, Malcolm X threw himself into the work of the NOI. In 1953, his efforts were rewarded and he became a minister in the movement. Malcolm X was a dynamic and energizing speaker. Even many Christian black people found his message engaging because he was at ease with ghetto life and directly pointed at the white people as those who were responsible for the difficult economic and social predicament in which they found themselves.

Malcolm X opened many NOI temples in northern cities. He also brought thousands of new converts into NOI because of his convincing oratory. For these reasons, Malcolm X became the most important disciple of Elijah Muhammad, the founder of NOI. At the heart of his political ideas were:

- The whole white race was evil.
- Racial integration was not the answer to the plight of the black people.
- Embracing white people after centuries of mistreatment was unnatural.
- Pride in one's racial identity and culture was key to success and happiness.

■ Break with NOI

Even though Malcolm X had essentially worshipped his mentor Elijah Muhammad, a series of factors led to his break from both the leader and the NOI. Other NOI disciples thought Malcolm X was gaining too much power which distracted attention away from Muhammad. They wanted him disciplined. Malcolm X, for his part, was upset by stories that he heard of their prophet, Elijah Muhammad, having relationships with at least six women and the several resulting children born outside marriage. He also disagreed with the non-political position of the NOI. Finally, his pilgrimage to Mecca in 1964 changed him. At Mecca, he saw a whole range of races freely worshipping the same god. Malcolm X soon began to question many of the teachings of his leader and he converted to Sunni Islam.

Back in the USA, Malcolm X publicly broke with Elijah Muhammad and founded the group Muslim Mosque Inc. Among the goals of this organization were to create a black-nationalist movement that was non-sectarian and to support civil rights groups such as SNCC. His outlook, that most civil rights leaders had being too accommodating with white people, and his views on race, in general, took a radical turn. Malcolm X had planned to meet Martin Luther King, Jr to discuss civil rights strategy but two days before the meeting on 21 February 1965 he was assassinated while giving a speech in New York City. The three gunmen who were arrested were NOI members.

ANALYSING A SOURCE

● In any given source, one can find a number of points raised by an author.

Read Source B and use the chart below to list which points note the differences between Martin Luther King, Jr and Malcolm X.

	Differences between Martin Luther King and Malcolm X
1	
2	
3	
4	
5	

Then answer the question which follows the source.

SOURCE B

Extract from Manning Marable, *Malcolm X: A Life of Reinvention*, Viking, New York, 2011, page 482. Marable was a professor of African American Studies at Columbia University.

There is now a tendency of historical revisionism, to interpret Malcolm X through the powerful lens of Dr. Martin Luther King, Jr.: that Malcolm was ultimately evolving into an integrationist, liberal reformer. This view is not only wrong, but unfair to both Malcolm and Martin. King saw himself, like Frederick Douglass, first and foremost as an American, who pursued civil rights and civic privileges enjoyed by other Americans. King struggled to erase the color bar of stigmatization and exclusion that had relegated racial minorities to second-class citizenship. As in the successful 2008 presidential campaign of Barack Obama, King wanted to convince white Americans that 'race doesn't matter' – in other words, the physical and color differences that appear to distinguish blacks from whites should be meaningless in the application of justice and equal rights.

In striking contrast, Malcolm perceived himself first and foremost as a black man, a person of African descent who happened to be a United States citizen. This was a crucial difference from King and other civil rights leaders. When he was a member of the Nation of Islam, Malcolm saw himself as a member of the tribe of Shabazz, the fictive Asiatic black clan invented by W.D. Fard. But in the final phases of his career, and especially in 1964–65, Malcolm linked his black consciousness to the ideological imperative of self-determination, the concept that all people have a natural right to decide for themselves their own destiny. Malcolm perceived black Americans as an oppressed nation-within-a-nation, with its own culture, social institutions, and group psychology … . At the end of his life he realized that black indeed could achieve representation and even power under America's constitutional system. But he always thought first and foremost about blacks' interests. Many blacks instinctively sensed this and loved him for it.

4 How did Martin Luther King, Jr and Malcolm X view themselves?

Lyndon B. Johnson (1908–73)

Revised

■ Lyndon B. Johnson

Of all US presidents, Lyndon B. Johnson led the US federal government into enacting the most far-reaching civil rights legislation. That a southerner from Texas should be the one to do so is even more surprising. Johnson was certainly a bundle of contradictions, paradoxes and moral certitudes. He was also a consummate politician who possessed a great supply of different tactics with which to bend opponents to his will. Still, Johnson's civil rights legacy was tarnished by his escalation of the US war in Vietnam which divided the country politically.

■ Early life

Johnson was born in Texas in 1908. One of his first jobs was as a schoolteacher. In this capacity, he saw the effects of poverty on his poor Mexican American students. This experience may later have helped shape his actions as president.

■ Johnson as a legislator

Johnson's legislative career spanned several decades:

- first elected to the US House of Representatives in 1937
- later won a seat in the US Senate in 1948.
- he then became the Senate Majority leader for the Democrats in 1955 when they became the majority political party in the Senate.

During this whole period, Johnson voted against every civil rights bill that came up for a vote. He sided with his fellow southern segregationists at every turn. This, however, was about to change.

In 1956, in reaction to the Supreme Court's *Brown* decision, almost every southern politician in Washington, DC signed the Southern Manifesto (see page 18). Johnson and two other southern senators did not sign the Manifesto. It is unclear whether or not Johnson refused to sign the document or wasn't asked to. By 1956, Johnson was already setting his sights on the presidency. If he had signed the Manifesto, he might have lost needed northern support forever.

What Johnson did do was to help pass President Eisenhower's 1957 Civil Rights Act. While the legislation was basically a toothless bill that did little to alter the dismal situation in the southern states, it was the first piece of legislation since Reconstruction, 82 years before, to address civil rights. Some historians have argued that this Act and the 1960 Civil Rights Act marked the first time in a very long time that the federal government was beginning to get involved in pressing for some change in allowing black people to vote in the Jim Crow South. Still, the number of black registered voters only increased by three per cent from 1957 to 1960. Southern senators allowed both bills to pass because they knew that they would not alter the *status quo* and that Johnson's appeal to those outside the South might increase, leading to the first southerner to become president in decades. But Johnson was outmanoeuvred at the Democratic national convention in 1960 by another candidate, John F. Kennedy. Johnson was offered and accepted the vice-presidential position. Johnson unexpectedly became president with Kennedy's assassination in November 1963.

■ The Great Society

When Johnson ran for the presidency in 1964, he announced a plan to create a 'Great Society' in the USA. He briefly outlined plans to end poverty in the country. Once the Democrats came to power in the 1964 electoral landslide, the depth and scope of the president's programme became clear when he announced in his State of the Union address in 1965, a whole raft of ideas that would impact education, healthcare, the arts, social welfare and transportation, among others. Many of his ideas were enacted during his presidency. They represented the greatest federal involvement in domestic affairs since Franklin Roosevelt's New Deals in the 1930s.

Martin Luther King, Jr and others did criticize Johnson's Great Society and loosely defined 'War on Poverty' because they thought the programmes were piecemeal and lacked any overarching co-ordination. Nonetheless, they did work with the president whenever they could. In terms of specific civil rights legislation, the 1964 Civil Rights Act and 1965 Voting Rights Act were major steps forward in providing equal access to public facilities and allowing all Americans the right to vote (see pages 40 and 48 for further detail). The ever-expanding, costly, and divisive war in Vietnam meant that much of Johnson's Great Society programmes fell by the wayside.

SUMMARIZING A SOURCE

● Question 16 of Paper 1 requires students to integrate knowledge from four sources and their own knowledge in response to a question about a topic from the one of the two case studies in Rights and protest.

● A successful response requires students to integrate summaries of sources.

● A good summary is based on the main ideas of a source.

● The main idea of a source can be identified using relevant content or identifying how relevant content is connected by a bigger idea or concept.

Answer the questions below with reference to Source C. After answering the questions, write a two-sentence summary of Source C.

SOURCE C

Extract from Nick Kotz, *Judgment Days: Lyndon Baines Johnson, Martin Luther King Jr., and the Laws that Changed America*, Houghton Mifflin Harcourt, 2006, page 92. The meeting described in the source took place in early 1962. Kotz is an American journalist and historian.

The civil rights leaders, having met previously to coordinate their own agendas, had expected to hear the president explain why he needed to compromise on the bill. He declared instead that he wanted the bill approved 'without a word or comma changed'. The black leaders also were surprised to learn that Johnson had another purpose for calling them to the White House. The president asked them to 'join him' as partners 'to help find the ways and means to mobilize support for the war on poverty', legislation for which he planned to send to Congress soon. As the discussion traveled around the table, all agreed that the problems of civil rights and poverty were inextricably connected. James Farmer emphasized the debilitating handicaps caused by illiteracy and point out that combating it was a 'vital part of the fight on discrimination'. Whitney Young called the high level of black unemployment, particularly among young black men, 'a national disgrace'. Martin Luther King called poverty 'a real catastrophe for Negroes' and declared an 'urgent need for action in education, remedial education, vocational training, and illiteracy'. If poor blacks and white alike were to enjoy their rights as Americans, the group agreed, help on a massive scale was needed.

When the leaders left the Oval Office and spoke to waiting reporters, it was clear that Johnson had skillfully broadened the civil rights agenda to include an attack on root problems suffered not just by racial minorities but by the poor of all races. There would be a dual war – against both poverty and racial discrimination – and Johnson had enlisted the nation's best known black leaders as his allies. Each one had pledged his support for Johnson's agenda …

5   Why were the black leaders surprised at the meeting with President Johnson?

6   What had Johnson hoped to accomplish in his meeting?

National Association for the Advancement of Colored People (NAACP)

■ Foundation and early years

One of the oldest and largest organizations that has fought for the civil rights of African Americans is the NAACP. It was formed in New York City in 1909 and its founders included such important activists as W.E.B. DuBois and Ida B. Wells. From the beginning, it was a biracial organization. The strategy of the NAACP was to publicize crimes against the African American community and to take legal steps to overturn laws that promoted racial segregation.

When Woodrow Wilson became president in 1913, he moved to segregate federal offices in the capital. The NAACP fought back and organized protest meetings that brought thousands together. Nonetheless, many departments were segregated along racial lines. During the years between the First and Second World Wars, the NAACP investigated and published a shocking report on the prevalence of lynching, particularly in the South.

■ NAACP and the courts

During the Second World War, NAACP membership grew from 50,000 to 450,000. With growing numbers, the NAACP began to embark on more and more lawsuits to force the government to enforce the 14th and 15th Amendments to the Constitution. Among the successful lawsuits were as follows:

Year	Case	Success
1944	*Smith v. Allwright*	The Supreme Court outlawed the Texas state law that had permitted all-white Democratic primaries
1950	*Sweatt v. Painter* and *McLaurin v. Oklahoma*	The dual law schools at University of Texas and the segregated facilities at the University of Oklahoma were deemed in violation of the 14th Amendment
1954	*Brown v. Board of Education of Topeka*	The NAACP brought together five cases of discrimination in education and argued that black students should be allowed to attend white schools. The Supreme Court unanimously agreed
1955	*Davis v. County School Board of Prince Edward County*, also known as *Brown II*	The Supreme Court ordered schools to desegregate 'with all deliberate speed'
1958	*Cooper v. Aaron*	The Supreme Court stated that its decisions must be followed even if they ran counter to state laws
1963	*NAACP v. Button*	The Supreme Court ruled in favour of the NAACP which had been targeted by Virginia

■ Thurgood Marshall

The NAACP's chief lawyer, Charles Houston, trained many black lawyers, including Thurgood Marshall. To help with the focus on legal challenges, the Legal Defense and Educational Fund was created in 1940 with Marshall as its head. He would later be the lead lawyer who successfully argued the 1950 and 1954 Supreme Court cases. Marshall became the first African American Supreme Court justice in 1967.

The strategy of trying to end desegregation through the court system was a slow and painful process. Other civil rights leaders took issue with this approach, preferring direct action and mass mobilization. Roy Wilkins, the secretary of the NAACP, fought with Martin Luther King, Jr over the best methods to achieve racial equality.

■ NAACP's relations with other groups

The NAACP did help other groups if they were facing difficult circumstances. It provided legal and financial aid to students arrested at sit-ins even though it did not agree with the methods used. It also posted bail for hundreds of Freedom Riders. Its actions sometimes met with harsh reprisals from state authorities. After helping to organize the Montgomery Bus Boycott, Alabama barred the NAACP from working in the state. It would take a Supreme Court decision to overturn this.

■ NAACP attacked

● Working for the NAACP could also be very dangerous.
● In addition to the countless beatings and imprisonment, NAACP workers lost their lives.
● In 1951, Harry Moore, a NAACP field secretary in Florida, was murdered.
● Medgar Evers, the head of the NAACP in Mississippi, was assassinated at his home in 1963.

■ Loss of prominence

The organization was one of the main organizers of the 1963 March on Washington for Jobs and Freedom. With the passage of the 1964 Civil Rights Act and the 1965 Voting Rights Act, though, the NAACP lost some of its earlier prominence and relevance. Both of these monumental legislative actions had resulted more from the direct action activities of the SCLC and SNCC than from NAACP litigation.

INTEGRATING KNOWLEDGE AND SOURCES

● Question 16 of Paper 1 requires students to integrate knowledge from four sources and their own understanding in response to a question about a topic from the one of the case studies.

Use Source D below and content from the opposite page in order to answer the question below.

SOURCE D

Extract from Taylor Branch, *Parting the Waters: America in the King Years, 1954–63*, Simon & Schuster, New York, 1988, pages 189–90. Branch is an American historian who wrote a massive three-volume series on Martin Luther King, Jr and the Civil Rights Movement.

King flew … to San Francisco to address the forty-seventh NAACP convention [1956]. Hundreds of delegates pressed upon him to shake his hand, including Medgar Evers, the NAACP field secretary in Mississippi. Evers invited King to Mississippi, saying that 'your presence would do more … than any' to raise hopes in his state. The idea of a mass movement by nearly fifty thousand Negroes in a single city [Montgomery] captivated the delegates, whose customary role in the NAACP was limited to support of the lawyers fighting segregation in court. Delegates on the convention floor drafted numerous resolutions in favor of nonviolent methods of the bus boycott. Wilkins and Thurgood Marshall opposed them in a protracted struggle that put King in the awkward positions of the insurrectionary guest. He tried to make himself as scarce as possible, but when reporters cornered him with questions about whether he thought nonviolent methods might help desegregate the schools, he replied that he had not thought about it much but that they probably could do so. This comment prompted an annoyed Thurgood Marshall to declare that school desegregation was men's work and should not be entrusted to children. Some reporters quoted him to the effect that King was a 'boy on a man's errand'. Wilkins worked more diplomatically to smother the threat of a runaway convention, finally engineering passage of a resolution calling merely for the executive board [of the NAACP] to give 'careful consideration' to the use of the Montgomery model.

7 Using the information from the opposite page and from Source D, explain why and how there were tensions between the NAACP and Martin Luther King, Jr.

Southern Christian Leadership Conference (SCLC)

■ Beginnings

The SCLC civil rights group was founded in January 1957, in the aftermath of the Montgomery Bus Boycott victory. Martin Luther King, Jr was chosen as its head and would remain so until his assassination in 1968. Many in the Civil Rights Movement saw the distinct need for one umbrella organization that could help organize and mobilize the various desegregation campaigns erupting across the South.

King brought together some of the finest and most respected activists into the organization:

- They included Ralph Abernathy, Ella Baker, Jesse Jackson, James Lawson, Joe Lowery, Diane Nash, Bayard Rustin, Fred Shuttlesworth and Andrew Young.
- Like most of these, many of the members of the SCLC were members of the southern African American clergy.
- Churches, both black and white, would play a large role in rallying support for the Civil Rights Movement.

■ SCLC ideology

It was no wonder that SCLC meetings were patterned on Sunday services given the religious makeup of the leadership. Similarly, much of the language used reflected biblical phraseology. Another key element in the group was the core philosophy of non-violent protest. Gandhi's non-violent civil disobedience campaigns had made a great impact on King and other SCLC ministers because the Indian nationalists did force the British to leave their country after many non-violent campaigns. The theory of non-violence was put to the test in Birmingham and Selma. Pacifism in the face of local and state violence proved successful and it was in no small measure that the Birmingham and Selma campaigns contributed greatly to the passing of the 1964 Civil Rights and 1965 Voting Rights Acts.

There was more to the SCLC's approach than just being passive, non-violent witnesses to the cruelties of the Jim Crow South. The SCLC encouraged its members to break what it considered to be unjust laws, thereby provoking white violence. In this sense, the group did exploit local black communities, many of whose members were jailed and beaten, for what it thought was the overall good.

■ SCLC and white people

The relationship between the SCLC and white people was also an issue for some. The SCLC believed that it needed more than just black support in order to destroy segregation. It actively enlisted the support of mostly northern white people. The SCLC understood that the southern white Americans had virtually all the economic and political power in the South and that it was necessary to go around them to make changes. This they did by appealing to sympathetic white people who were appalled by the repression they could see on their nightly television newscasts. Many white people, in turn, pressured their representatives in Congress to act to stop the violence.

■ Northern influences

The SCLC was more than a southern organization. While it was certainly rooted in the South, it received guidance from northern activists such as Bayard Rustin. Its leader, Dr King, also represented both sections of the country. King had completed much of his education in the South, but did his PhD at Boston University in Massachusetts, in the North.

■ Challenges

The SNCC faced serious challenges in the 1950s and 1960s. The internal workings of the group were known to be chaotic. Crippling inefficiencies and unreliability in organizing campaigns led to harsh criticism. On the other hand, some analysts saw these characteristics not only as negatives. The group had the capacity for spontaneity and quick flexibility. It could react to change on the ground rapidly, something that a more conservative group such as the NAACP could not do.

Serious disagreements with the NAACP and the SCLC over basic goals and strategy also reflected deep splits within the Civil Rights Movement, splits that could not be easily overcome. By the mid-1960s these disagreements led to the virtual disintegration of any semblance of a united front and it became more difficult to have similar goals, let alone common strategy.

MAKING INFERENCES

- Sometimes when working with sources, not all of the information presented is clearly stated.
- It can be necessary to read between the lines or to make inferences from the information presented.

Read Source E closely and then answer the question that follows.

SOURCE E

Extract from the founding document of the Southern Negro Leaders Conference on Transportation and Non-violent Integration. At the January 1957 meeting, 60 black leaders from 29 communities of ten southern states met in Atlanta, Georgia. In August, the group was renamed the Southern Christian Leadership Conference (http:/kingencyclopedia.stanford.edu/ primarydocuments/Vol4/11-Jan-1957_AStatementToTheSouth.pdf).

… Even the Congress of our land is shackled. It is unable to enact urgently needed social legislation. Federal aid to education and increased social security bills for the benefit of white and Negro people die in congressional committees because the division over civil rights permits a small minority to capture and control the legislative branch of our national government.

Thus the entire nation suffers because our democratic vitality is sapped by the civil rights issue. This is even more true of the South. In her unwillingness to accept the Negro as a human being, the South has chosen to remain undeveloped, poorly educated and emotionally warped.

Through recent Supreme Court decisions, declaring that discrimination based on race violates the Constitution, the issue has been joined. There is no turning back. The nation must now face the reality that American can never realize its vast economic, social and political potential until the struggle for civil rights has been decisively won.

We are convinced that the great majority of white southerners are prepared to accept and abide by the Supreme Law of the Land. They, like us, want to be law-abiding citizens. Yet a small but determined minority resorts to threats, bodily assaults, cross-burnings, bombing, shooting and open defiance of the law in an attempt to force us to retreat. But we cannot in clear conscience turn back. We have no moral choice but to continue the struggle, not for ourselves alone but for all America. We have the God given duty to help save ourselves and our white brothers from tragic self-destruction in the quagmire of racial hate. We must continue to stand firm for our right to be first class citizens. Even in the face of death, we have no other choice … .

8 In what ways does the document suggest that the issues confronting the USA do not solely affect the South?

MIND MAP

Create a mind map on the SCLC using information from the preceding page.

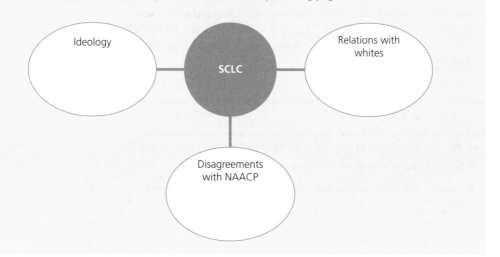

Student Nonviolent Coordinating Committee (SNCC)

Revised

Founding

In April 1960, at the urging of Ella Baker, the executive director of the SCLC, more than 300 students met at Shaw College in Raleigh, North Carolina. She hoped the African American students from 56 colleges from twelve southern states, as well as some white students from northern colleges, could create a group-centred and youthful organization. The new group would be unlike other more established groups such as the NAACP and the SCLC.

At this meeting, Martin Luther King, Jr spoke. He was followed by James Lawson. Lawson had participated in the Nashville sit-ins. The students responded much more enthusiastically to him because he represented young activists engaged in direct action rather than a slower, more traditional approach. Baker also spoke and she encouraged the students to fight against injustice in housing, employment, healthcare and voting. They started a mass movement that tackled all of these issues.

SNCC campaigns

Among the many protests and campaigns the SNCC were involved in were:

- 1961: the Freedom Rides
- 1961–3: Freedom Summer and voter registration drives in Mississippi
- 1961: Albany Movement
- 1963: March on Washington for Freedom and Jobs; John Lewis, leader of SNCC spoke there and said, 'We want our freedom and we want it now!'
- 1964: helped form the Mississippi Freedom Democratic Party (MFDP)
- 1965: March from Selma to Montgomery

Mississippi Freedom Democratic Party (MFDP) and the 1964 Democratic Convention

During the 1964 election year, Mississippi's 68-member delegation to the Democratic Convention, where the presidential candidate would be chosen, was all white. SNCC and others formed the MFDP to provide an alternative group to represent Mississippi's Democratic voters. President Johnson did not want the national party to be torn apart by racial division and he did not want to risk losing southern support. The MFDP was forced to accept a compromise. The all-white delegation would be the official one. Two MFDP members would be given non-voting and non-speaking seats in the delegation. They were also promised that before the 1968 convention, they would be able to vote and elect black representatives. Dr King and other SCLC leaders agreed to this solution. For the SNCC, the whole affair left a bitter taste and they thought they had been betrayed. Many felt that they could not trust the national Democratic Party or white liberals any longer.

SNCC infighting

This sense of betrayal was furthered during the Selma campaign in 1965. During the second of three marches there, the 'ministers' march', the protesters turned back when they reached police lines instead of challenging the authorities. This had secretly been agreed to ahead of the march, but the SNCC were not informed.

Bitter infighting erupted in the SNCC afterwards. Many members felt that the non-violent approach was no longer working or taking far too long for real change and that the inclusion of whites in the group was a distraction. In 1965, Stokely Carmichael and other SNCC activists in Alabama started the all-black Lowndes Country Freedom Organization. Lowndes was chosen because even though 80% of the population was black, not a single black person was registered to vote. The group used a black panther as their symbol.

SNCC was disbanded in 1967 as the civil rights movement splintered and violent upheavals occurred in inner cities across the USA.

SOURCE F

Student Nonviolent Coordinating Committee founding statement, adopted by the Southwide Youth Leadership Conference, Shaw University, Raleigh, NC, 15–17 April 1960 (www.crmvet.org/docs/sncc1.htm).

We affirm the philosophical or religious ideal of nonviolence as the foundation of our purpose, the presupposition of our belief, and the manner of our action.

Nonviolence, as it grows from the Judeo-Christian tradition, seeks a social order of justice permeated by love. Integration of human endeavor represents the crucial first step towards such a society.

Through nonviolence, courage displaces fear. Love transcends hate. Acceptance dissipates prejudice; hope ends despair. Faith reconciles doubt. Peace dominates war. Mutual regards cancel enmity. Justice for all overthrows injustice. The redemptive community supersedes immoral social systems.

By appealing to conscience and standing on the moral nature of human existence, nonviolence nurtures the atmosphere in which reconciliation and justice become actual possibilities.

Although each local group in this movement must diligently work out the clear meaning of this statement of purpose, each act or phase of our corporate effort must reflect a genuine spirit of love and good-will.

COMPARING AND CONTRASTING SOURCES

- The following activity is designed to help students identify similarities and differences between sources.
- Similarities and differences should focus on significant knowledge, not basic statements, dates, and so on.
- Differences may identify significant knowledge or themes raised in one source that are not found in the other source.

Use Source E on page 63 and Source F above. Identify similarities and differences and record them in the table below.

	Source E	Source F	Explanation
Similarity 1			
Similarity 2			
Similarity 3			
Difference 1			
Difference 2			
Difference 3			

WRITING A COMPARE AND CONTRAST RESPONSE

- Take the information from the table from the activity above and write a response to the question below.
- Review the examples of effective sentence structures given below before writing your response.
- A focused response will consist of six statements, one per similarity or difference.
- It also will completely address one demand, compare for example, before addressing the other demand, contrast.
- Normally, provide one paragraph for comparisons and one paragraph for differences.

Sample sentence structures for comparing and contrasting sources

Comparing
- Both Source E and Source F ...
- Source E identifies ... so does Source F with '...'
- Source E claims ... similarly Source F states ...

Contrasting
- Source E emphasizes ... but Source F focuses on ...
- While Source E asserts ... Source F claims ...
- Source E examines ... on the other hand, Source F refers to ...

9   Compare and contrast how Source E and Source F explain the reasons behind each group's creation.

Nation of Islam (NOI)

Revised

■ Founding and early years

The NOI is one of the oldest Muslim organizations in the USA and its members are all African American. It was founded in Chicago in 1930 by Wallace D. Fard Muhammad. Muhammad mysteriously disappeared and the group was then led by Elijah Muhammad, the founder's main disciple.

Elijah Muhammad had been influenced by black nationalists such as Marcus Garvey as well as Wallace D. Fard Muhammad. In addition to the Muslim holy book, the Qu'ran, the NOI used *The Supreme Wisdom*, a collection of written lessons passed down from Muhammad to Elijah Muhammad, as central texts.

During the Second World War, the NOI was put under FBI surveillance because the group was thought to be collaborating with Japan. Elijah Muhammad and other members of the group went to prison for refusing to register for the US Army. The NOI claimed that their beliefs prevented them from participating in an American war.

■ Core NOI beliefs

Among the core beliefs of the NOI were:

- The black man was the original man. All other races were descended from black people.
- Black people came from the tribe of Shabazz in Asia. White people were created by an evil scientist named Yacub and were devils.
- There is no God but Allah.
- Elijah Muhammad was a prophet.
- Separation, not integration, with white people was the path forward.
- The race problems would be solved by divine intervention.

■ Impact of Malcolm X

The NOI was a fairly small religious sect until the charismatic Malcolm X became the spokesman of the group. His energy and convincing speeches helped the group expand greatly. New religious temples were opened in many cities, particularly outside the Baptist-dominated South, and thousands of African Americans converted to Islam.

■ Appeal of NOI

What the converts found appealing was that the religion:

- stressed the importance of self-help and self-sufficiency
- preached self-respect
- provided schools for children and adults
- had black-owned stores
- was free of drugs and crime
- offered protection and salvation from the 'white devils'.

■ Elijah Muhammad and Malcolm X split

Malcolm X eventually became disenchanted with NOI's lack of action for social and political change. This included the non-engagement with the Civil Rights Movement. He also knew that other Muslim groups found some of NOI's basic beliefs to be bizarre in the extreme. The break reached a point when, in answer to a question about Kennedy's assassination, he replied in an offhand manner that suggested that violence in the USA was to be expected, especially given the violence spread by America overseas, and that he was even a bit happy about the assassination.

Elijah was quick to condemn his follower and punished him by ordering him to stop preaching in his mosque for 90 days. He also said that, 'The president of the country is our president, too,' even though he told NOI members not to vote in US elections. Not long after, Malcolm X left the NOI.

■ Death of Elijah Muhammad

The group would remain controversial after the mid-1960s. It continued to preach separate development until the death of Elijah Muhammad in 1975. Thereafter, it repudiated his racial ideology and became much more of a mainstream Islamic group, similar to Sunni Islam.

IDENTIFYING RELEVANT CONTENT FROM AN ILLUSTRATION

- Question 13 contains two parts (13a and 13b), both of which test your understanding of two different sources.
- Question 13b is always a non-text source, that is, a political cartoon, a propaganda poster, a photograph, and so on.
- Students are asked to identify two main messages or points from the source.

Examine the following illustration from Source G and then answer the following questions that focus on identifying relevant content.

10 How are white and black people portrayed in Source G?

11 What does the cartoon suggest about black unity?

SOURCE G

Illustration from the *Muhammad Speaks* newspaper, December 1961. *Muhammad Speaks* was an official NOI publication. Elijah Muhammad is in the centre of the picture and the sheet before him reads, 'MUHAMMAD'S ECONOMIC BLUEPRINT FOR THE BLACKMAN'.

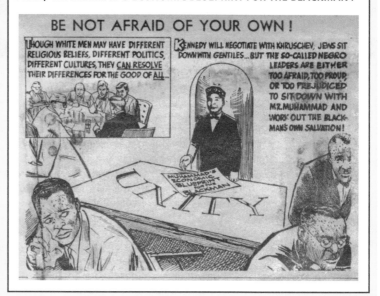

CONNECTING ORIGIN, PURPOSE AND CONTENT TO VALUE AND LIMITATION

Use Source H below to identify origin, purpose and content and to connect them to value and limitation for a historian studying the key group, the Nation of Islam:

- Use the table to record your thoughts.
- In the first column, record key information about the source. In Value, connect the key information to how it is valuable to a historian.
- In Limitations, connect the key information to how it has limitations for a historian.

SOURCE H

Extract from Malcolm X's speech to a mostly black Christian audience in New York City in 1963. Quoted in David Howard-Pitney, *Martin Luther King Jr., Malcolm X, and the Civil Rights Struggle of the 1950s and 1960s.* Bedford, Boston, 2004, page 70.

… The Honorable Elijah Muhammad says a desegregated theater, a desegregated lunch counter won't solve our problems. Better jobs won't solve our problems. An integrated cup of coffee isn't sufficient pay for four hundred years of slave labor. He also says that a better job, a better job in the white man's industry or economy is, at best, only a temporary solution. He says that the only lasting and permanent solution is complete separation on some land that we can call our own. Therefore, the Honorable Elijah Muhammad says that this problem can be solved and solved forever just by sending our people back to our own homeland or back to our own people, but that this government should provide the transportation plus everything else we need to get started again in our own country. This government should give us everything we need in the form of machinery, material, and finance – enough to last for twenty to twenty-five years until we can become an independent people and an independent nation in our own land … .

And in my conclusion I repeat: We want no part of integration with this wicked race that enslaved us. We want complete separation from this wicked race of devils.

	Key information	Value	Limitations
Type of source			
Date created			
Perspective issues			
Purpose			
Content			

Source booklet

Read Sources I and J below and answer question 15 in the accompanying question paper.

SOURCE I

Extract from *The Autobiography of Malcolm X*, Penguin Books, New York, 1968, pages 387–8. The book was jointly written with Alex Haley. Here Malcolm X comments on the 1963 March on Washington.

The marchers had been instructed to bring no signs – signs were provided. They had been told to sing one song: 'We Shall Overcome'. They had been told *how* to arrive, *when, where* to arrive, *where* to assemble, when to *start* marching, the *route* to march. First-aid stations were strategically located – even where to *faint*! Yes, I was there. I observed that circus. Who ever heard of angry revolutionists all harmonizing 'We Shall Overcome … Suum Day …' while tripping and swaying along arm-in-arm with the very people they were supposed to be angrily revolting against? …

In a subsequent press poll, not one Congressman or senator with a previous record of opposition to civil rights said he had changed his views. What did anyone expect? How was a one-day 'integrated' picnic going to counter-influence these representatives of injustice rooted deep in the psyche of the American white man for four hundred years?

The very fact that millions, white and black, believed in this monumental farce is another example of how much this country goes in for the surface glossing over … instead of truly dealing with its deep-rooted problems.

SOURCE J

Extract from E.W. Kenworthy's article, '200,000 March for Civil Rights in Orderly Washington Rally; President Sees Gain for Negro', in the *New York Times*, 29 August 1963. Kenworthy was a Washington correspondent for the *New York Times*.

More than 200,000 Americans, most of them black but many of them white, demonstrated here today for a full and speedy program of civil rights and equal job opportunities.

It was the greatest assembly for redress of grievances that this capital has ever seen …

But if the crowd was good-natured, the underlying tone was one of dead seriousness. The emphasis was on 'freedom' and 'now'. At the same time the leaders emphasized, paradoxically but realistically, that the struggle was just beginning.

On Capitol Hill, opinion was divided about the impact of the demonstration in stimulating Congressional action on civil rights legislation …

Senator Everett McKinley Dirksen of Illinois, the Republican leader, said he thought the demonstration would be neither an advantage nor a disadvantage to the prospects for the civil rights bill …

Harshest of all the speakers was John Lewis, chairman of the Student Nonviolent Coordinating Committee.

'My friends,' he said, 'let us not forget that we are involved in a serious social revolution. But by and large American politics is dominated by politicians who build their career on immoral compromising and ally themselves with open forms of political, economic and social exploitation.'

Sample question and answer

Below is a sample answer. Read it and the comments around it.

- Question 15 of Paper 1 requires students to compare and contrast two sources.
- The comparing and contrasting of the sources should focus on the content, analyses and/or interpretations of the sources.
- When comparing sources, students should identify and explain similar content found in the sources.
- When contrasting sources, students should identify and explain differences in the sources.
- The question is worth 6 marks. Three similarities and three differences are needed to achieve full marks for the comparing portion of this question.
- You should spend about fifteen minutes answering this question.

15 Compare and contrast how Sources I and J interpret the 1963 March on Washington.

Sources I and J share a number of views regarding the 1963 March on Washington. Source I states that members of Congress had not changed their views after the march. In other words, the march had little impact on the legislative branch. Source J supports this. The Republican leader, Dirksen, said the march had little impact on whether or not the civil rights bill would pass. Another area of similarity is the racial makeup of the crowd. Source I mentions the 'integrated picnic' while Source J states that there were both blacks and whites attending the march. The two sources also agree on the depth of the problems facing the USA. In Source I, Malcolm X sees the country as not willing to face the terrible challenges. Source J supports this. John Lewis mentions that the political structure in the USA is dominated by those who continually make immoral compromises and who work with 'exploitation' on many levels. Finally, the two sources agree that the march was 'orderly'. Source J makes this point in the article's headline, while Source I discusses how every little action was choreographed at the demonstration.

> There are running comparisons throughout.

> Comparisons and contrasts have been separated into two paragraphs.

However, the two sources do contain significant differences. Source I believes the event was a gigantic 'circus', while Source J calls the demonstration 'the greatest assembly for redress of grievances' and that it was a very serious affair. Furthermore, Source I claims that the event was planned at every step of the way. Source J, on the other hand, makes no mention of this but only states that the day was devoted to pushing civil rights forward. Finally, the importance of the event was also viewed differently in the two sources. Source I viewed the March on Washington as a great farce, while Source J saw the event as very serious and that it marked the beginning of the struggle for economic and social justice.

> There is appropriate use of language, especially in connected sources of points. Examples of words that help build linkage are 'both', 'while', 'however' and 'on the other hand'.

6/6. This response earns full marks because it provides four comparisons and three contrasts. There is running commentary throughout and each comparison and contrast is backed up with evidence. Selective use of quotations is used from the sources to reinforce the answer.

Exam practice

Now it's your turn to take a mock exam.

Read Sources M–P below and answer questions 13–16 in the accompanying question paper. The sources and questions relate to Case study 1: The Civil Rights Movement in the United States 1954–65 – the role and significance of key actors/groups: Student Nonviolent Coordinating Committee (SNCC).

SOURCE M

Charles Sherrod was 22 when he went to Albany, Georgia in 1961 to work as a SNCC organizer. This is an extract from the untitled and undated account that Sherrod wrote a year or two later. Quoted in Clayborne Carson, ed., *The Eyes on the Prize Civil Rights Reader*, Penguin Books, New York, 1991, page 138.

The population of Albany was in the first days of our stay here, very apprehensive. We had told many that our intention was to organize a voter-registration campaign, the first step of which was to establish an office … The first obstacle to remove was the mental block in the minds of those who wanted to move but were unable for fear that we were not who we said we were. But when people began to hear us in churches, social meetings, on the streets, in the pool halls, lunchrooms, nightclubs, and other places where people gather, they began to open us a bit … We explained to them that we had stopped school because we felt compelled to do so since so many of us were in chains. We explained further that there were worse chains than jail and prison. We referred to the system that imprisons men's minds and robs them of creativity. We mocked the system that teaches men to be good Negroes instead of good men.

SOURCE N

Extract from 'Ain't Scared of Your Jails (1960–61)' by Clayborne Carson, a chapter introduction in Clayborne Carson, ed., *The Eyes on the Prize Civil Rights Reader*, Penguin Books, New York, 1991, page 107. Carson is a professor of History at Stanford University and director of the Martin Luther King Jr. Research and Education Institute.

The increasing confidence of the student activists was evident in a new organization, the Student Nonviolent Coordinating Committee (SNCC), and in a new wave of protests called Freedom Rides.

The formation of SNCC followed the sit-ins by only a few months and not only solidified student involvement in the movement but placed students in leadership roles … Influenced by James Lawson, a divinity student at Vanderbilt University with a philosophical commitment to nonviolent direct action, the students began to develop an organization that would channel their concerns and energy. What emerged was a coordinating committee that operated independently of other established civil rights organizations and relied on strong local leadership. The formation of SNCC helped transform the student movement from one that emphasized small-scale protests to a sustained force that would challenge racism throughout American society.

SOURCE O

'Freedom Day' in Selma, Alabama, 7 October 1963. SNCC members arrested. Photo by photojournalist Danny Lyon of Magnum Photos.

SOURCE P

Extract from 'Judge Elliott Refuses U.S. Request to Restrain Terrell County Law Officer Threats', 15 August 1962, *Atlanta Daily World*. The *Atlanta Daily World* was an African American newspaper based in Atlanta, Georgia.

A federal judge Tuesday turned down a Justice Department request for a temporary restraining order barring law enforcement officers from threatening prospective Negro voters.

Justice Department attorneys went before Judge Robert Elliott Monday to accuse two Georgia sheriffs of disrupting two Negro voter registration meetings … The government also had asked Elliott to halt prosecution of two representatives of the pro-integration Student Non-Violent Coordinating Committee, SNCC. The SNCC representatives were arrested on vagrancy [homeless] charges when they accompanied a group of Negroes who sought to register to vote at the courthouse in Dawson, Georgia …

The government charged that Sherriff Mathews and others disrupted two voter registration meetings recently in Sasser at Negro Baptist churches. The government complaint said a group of white men barged into one of the meetings and threatened Negroes with physical harm. It asked that the defendants be forbidden to intimidate prospective voters by disrupting meetings, threatening violence, discharging Negro employees or committing violence. In turning down the request for the restraining order, Elliott said that 'persons registering now could not in any event vote in the forthcoming election'.

Elliott is the federal judge who heard the City of Albany's request for a court order which would restrain Negroes from staging anti-segregation demonstrations. He now has that case under advisement.

13 a What, according to Source P, was the Justice Department asking Judge Elliott to do? [3]

   b What does Source O suggest about Freedom Day in Selma? [2]

14 With reference to its origin, purpose and content, analyse the value and limitations of Source P for a historian studying the challenges faced by SNCC and the US Justice Department. [4]

15 Compare and contrast what Sources M and N reveal about SNCC's activities. [6]

16 Using the sources and your own knowledge, evaluate the role SNCC played in the Civil Rights Movement in the early 1960s. [9]

4 Nature and characteristics of discrimination

Segregation in legislation before 1948 and South African political parties

■ South African background

South Africa in the first half of the twentieth century was a deeply divided country. The majority of the population, roughly 68%, was black, while white people, divided between descendants of the early Dutch settlers and those from Britain, made up twenty per cent. The Dutch were known as Afrikaners. The rest were of Indian origin or of mixed racial backgrounds, known as coloureds. Many discriminatory laws had been passed by the British-dominated government up to the Second World War.

■ Segregation laws before apartheid

While the white Africans tried to exclude the black Africans, they nonetheless needed their labour, whether in the mines or their homes or their fields. Certainly, one goal was to control freedom of movement and to create a docile workforce. Among the measures taken by various South African governments were:

- 1911 Mine and Works Act: this kept Africans from most skilled jobs in the mines, leaving them to do the hard labour without prospects of advancement.
- 1911 Natives' Labour Regulation Act: one way for the authorities to control the movement of Africans was to fingerprint them and force them to carry pass books which allowed them to enter their areas of work. Without the pass book, an African would be fined and jailed if caught.
- 1913 Natives Land Act: black Africans were restricted to seven per cent of the total land in the country. These areas were known as native reserves or homelands. Because they were often overcrowded and located on infertile soil, many Africans were forced to work for white people to support their families.
- 1923 Natives (Urban Areas) Act: Africans who worked in the mines or factories were forced to live in townships, usually located on the outskirts of cities. They were expected to leave the townships when their contracts were over. The only Africans who were supposed to be in the cities were those working as domestic servants.
- 1924 Industrial Conciliation Act: African workers were restricted in joining or organizing trade unions. They had few rights as workers.
- 1927 Native Administration Act: The Department of Native Affairs was created to deal with all issues regarding the Africans. They were separated from other groups in South African society.
- 1936 Native Trust and Land Act: the native reserves were expanded from 7% to 13.6% of South Africa's land. Africans were forbidden to purchase any property outside the reserves.
- 1936 Representation of the Natives Act: before 1936, about 10,000 Africans were allowed to vote in the Cape if they owned a certain amount of land. The Act stripped them of this right and they now had no rights of permanent residence outside the tribal reserves. A smaller group of the African elite, some 4000, were permitted to vote for four white representatives who were supposed to represent their interests in the Senate.

EXAMINING THE CONTENT OF A SOURCE

- Question 14 of Paper 1 requires students to evaluate the value and limitations of a source based on its origin, purpose and content.
- Content refers to the information contained in a source.
- Content value comes from information in the source that supports the topic being examined.
- Content limitation comes from information in the source that does not support the topic being examined. Content limitation also can result from information found in the source that addresses only part of the scope of the topic being examined.

For the questions below, refer to Source A. The following questions are designed to make connections between the content of a source and how it affects value or limitation. Use the topic: for a historian studying South African political views.

SOURCE A

Extract from the speech by Jan Smuts, 'The racial and moral axioms', 1917. Quoted in David Gordon, *Apartheid in South Africa: A Brief History with Documents*, Bedford/St. Martin's, Boston, 2017, page 33. Smuts was prime minister of South Africa 1919–24 and 1939–48.

We have felt more and more that if we are to solve our native question it is useless to try to govern black and white in the same system, to subject them to the same institutions of government and legislation. They are different not only in colour but in minds and in political capacity, and their political institutions should be different, while always proceeding on the basis of self-government … .We have now legislation before the Parliament of the Union in which an attempt is made to put into shape these ideas I am talking of, and to create all over South Africa, wherever there are nay considerable native communities, independent self-governing institutions for them. Instead of mixing up black and white in the old haphazard way, which instead of lifting up the black degraded the white, we are now trying to lay down a policy of keeping them apart as much as possible in our institutions. In land ownership settlement and forms of government we are trying to keep them apart, and in laying down in outline a general policy which it may take a hundred years to work out, but which in the end may be the solution to our native problem …. The native will, of course, be free to go and to work in the white areas, but as far as possible the administration of white and black areas will be separated, and such that each will be satisfied and developed according to its own proper lines.

1 Why does Smuts think natives and whites would be better off if they were separated?
2 How are Smuts' views on race of value for a historian studying South African political views?
3 What are the limitations of this extract?

CONTRASTING TWO SOURCES

- Question 15 asks you to compare and contrast two sources.

Read the following source and find three differences between the views in the source and those from Source A.

SOURCE B

Extract from Nancy Clark and William Worger, *South Africa: The Rise and Fall of Apartheid*, third edition, Routledge, Abingdon, 2016, pages 20–1. Clark and Worger are US historians who have written extensively on African history.

Racial discrimination in South Africa in the years following Union in 1910 and preceding the institution of apartheid in 1948 was enforced through a policy of segregation. Although implemented to varying degrees throughout the new country, the policy of segregation generally separated races to the benefit of those of European descent to the detriment of those of African descent. Segregation policies affected the rights of Africans to own land, to live or travel where they chose and to enjoy job security. While segregation was not as sweeping or inclusive as apartheid, neither was it an informal system of discrimination. Segregation policies that increasingly limited African rights were implemented through a series of laws passed during the first half of the twentieth century, and which were often enforced with great brutality … .

Segregation policies attempted to protect white political and economic interests while at the same time drawing Africans increasingly into the country's economy as the chief source of labour … . [Africans] were to be recruited in the rural areas, fingerprinted and issued with a 'pass' allowing them to enter cities, and if they broke their employment contract or stayed in the urban areas beyond the length of the contract, they were to be arrested and forced to do hard labour for up to two months.

4 What three differences could you find?

1948 Elections

Revised ☐

■ South African political parties

South Africa was a British dominion and thus controlled by Britain politically. The British appointed a governor general and many of the 50 senators in the Senate. The members of the House of Assembly were usually elected every five years. Among the major political parties before the 1948 elections were:

- The United Party: this was dominated by English-speaking South Africans who wished to continue being closely linked to Britain.
- South African Party: similar to the United Party, its members favoured close ties to Britain and the continuation of segregation policies.
- National Party: the party was comprised mostly of Afrikaners who wished to impose apartheid and to push for independence from Britain.
- Purified National Party: this was created in 1934 in opposition to the merger of the National Party and the South African Party. It would later turn into the Reunited National Party or RNP.

They were hardliners and opposed the United Party in Parliament.

■ National Party platform

In 1948, the Reunited National Party (RNP), in a coalition with the Afrikaner Party, defeated the United Party. The RNP had run a platform on the following issues:

- After the Second World War, returning soldiers found it difficult to find jobs. Many black people had taken their jobs for less money.
- The increase in the number of strikes and protests by black people shocked and frightened many Afrikaners.
- During the war, thousands of black people had moved to the cities from the rural areas to find work in the war industries. White farmers wanted the cheap labour they had had before the war.
- Racial mixing was something that should avoided at all costs.
- The United Party would increase the civil rights of black people.

While the victory was a narrow one, 79 seats versus 71 seats, it was enough to begin a policy of racial separation that would last for the next four decades.

The RNP absorbed the smaller Afrikaner party and renamed itself the National Party. D.F. Malan became the prime minister. Among the aims of the new government were to impose a system to ensure white supremacy through a total system of apartheid or separateness and to end all political ties with Britain and form an independent republic.

■ Beginnings of apartheid

Even though there was no master plan for imposing apartheid, the new government started carrying out a series of racial policies and the apartheid began. Among the measures taken were:

- The state employed more and more white people, especially in the civil service and the railways. The number of Africans working for the government decreased. The Afrikaner males who were hired lent their support to the National Party in gratitude for their jobs.
- 'Europeans only' signs began to appear on Cape Town trains.
- Plans were announced to control the spread of African shanty towns in urban areas.
- Malan announced that universities would be segregated.

■ Resistance to apartheid

The Africans, led by the African National Congress (ANC), and especially its younger members who belonged to the ANC Youth League or ANCYL, responded to these government moves. In 1949, they issued their programme, known as the Basic Policy. It stated that:

- They rejected what the Afrikaners termed *baasskap* or boss-ship, meaning white superiority and domination.
- Mass and direct action was needed to stop further legislative attacks on their communities.
- They were proud to be African and were not inferior to white people.
- African nationalism throughout the continent should be supported to counter British, French and Portuguese colonialism.

Shortly thereafter, the ANC formally accepted the Basic Policy as a core element of the party platform.

EXAMINING A SOURCE FOR ITS PURPOSE

● Question 14 asks you to determine the value and limitations of a source through its origin, purpose and content.

Read the source below and answer the questions that follow.

SOURCE C

Extract from a *New York Times* article, 'South African Hints Racial Registration', 17 November 1948.

Addressing the Transvaal congress of Nationalist party delegates today, Prime Minister Daniel F. Malan dealt principally with racial relations and foreshadowed the introduction of a system of 'racial registration.' He said:

'If a person has black blood as near as one grandparent, then he will have to be classified as a non-European. On each person's identity card will have to be indicated the race to which he belongs, and he will have to remain a member of that race. Otherwise how could mixed marriages be prevented?

Political feeling is rising to such pitch that when the name of former Prime Minister Jan Christiaan Smuts was mentioned today at the opening of the congress delegates shouted 'hang him!' and 'intern him!' There were loud cheers when the Minister of Lands Johannes G. Strydom, declared: 'Smuts is no longer a son of South Africa'.

5   Who produced this source?
6   Why was this source produced?
7   How is the purpose of this source valuable for a historian studying the introduction of apartheid?

MIND MAP

Create a mind map using the information from Source C and the text on the preceding page.

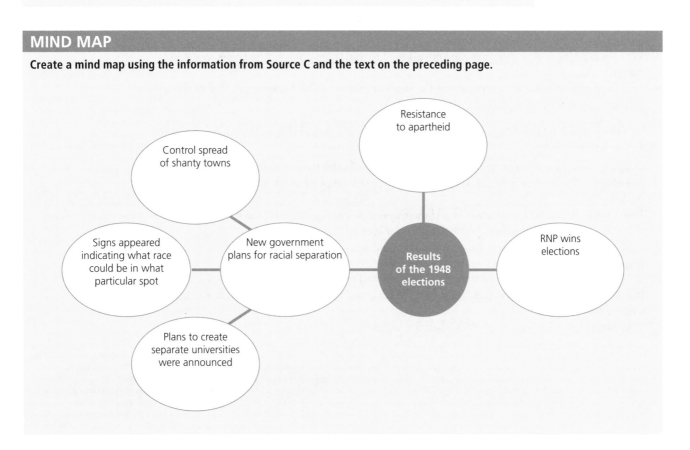

Petty and grand apartheid

◼ The appeal of apartheid to white people

Soon after the National Party came to power in 1948, it made good on its promises to segregate the nation to the greatest extent possible. A comprehensive set of laws were passed to this end. White South Africans, often referred to as Europeans, stood to gain much from apartheid as it guaranteed them a large slice of South Africa's wealth. Well-paid jobs and very good living conditions were part of the enticement for cooperating with the new regime.

The laws were designed to keep physical contacts between the races to a minimum and institutionalize discrimination.

◼ Petty and grand apartheid

The laws that were enacted are usually categorized as petty apartheid and grand apartheid. Petty apartheid referred to the laws that impacted day-to-day life. For example, separate beaches, restaurants and toilet facilities would fall under this category. There was a never-ending application of these laws. Grand apartheid involved the loss of political and land rights.

Among the chief petty apartheid laws were:

- 1949 Prohibition of Mixed Marriages Act: marriages between people of different races were illegal.
- 1950 Immorality Act: sexual relations between members of different races were illegal.
- 1951 Bantu Building Workers Act: Africans were limited in the skilled jobs they could have in the construction industry.
- 1952 Native Laws Amendment Act: replaced pass books with reference books. Africans had to carry these at all times.
- 1953 Bantu Education Act: control of education moved from the Ministry of Education to the Ministry for Native Affairs. Church-run schools no longer received funding from the state and many were forced to close. Much of the curriculum focused on vocational training instead of preparing African students for further education.
- 1953 Native Labour Act: Africans were not allowed to join trade unions. They could not take part in strikes.
- 1953 Separate Amenities Act: this was at the heart of petty apartheid legislations. Public spaces and services were divided according to race.

Grand apartheid laws had great consequences for where Africans could live and how they would be classified. These included:

- 1950 Population Registration Act: all South Africans had to be registered and separated in one of the following four categories: European or white, Asian, Coloured, and Native or Black African.
- 1950 Group Areas Act: registration of all land ownership was required and the government was given the authority to designate particular areas for specific racial groups.
- 1951 Native Resettlement Act: the government could move Africans from the Johannesburg region to anywhere it so chose.
- 1951 Bantu Authorities Act: Africans were only allowed to live in their tribal reserves unless they had work permits. Tribal reserves were to be governed by those tribal leaders chosen by the white government.
- 1958 Bantu Self-Government Act: this laid the foundation for the creation of eight Bantustans.

EXAMINING THE CONTENT OF A SOURCE

- The first question of Paper 1 contains two parts, 13a and 13b, both of which test understanding of two different sources.
- Question 13a is always an excerpt from a written source.
- Students are asked to identify at least three main points from the source.

Read Source D and then answer the following questions that focus on identifying relevant content.

SOURCE D

Extract from a speech by Senator Dr Verwoerd in which he addressed his peers, 3 September 1948. Verwoerd quoted from his party's published policy of apartheid, as well as offering his own conclusions about the racial situation in South Africa (http://hendrikverwoerd.blogspot.com/2010/12/september-3-1948-policy-of-apartheid-hf.html).

When we come to 'Social Welfare and Public Health [in the National Party programme],' you find that it is stated here:

'There must be separate residential areas for European and non-Europeans, and as far as possible this principle of apartheid must also be applied to the various non-European racial groups in their relationships towards one another, such as coloured people, Indians and Natives.' …

'The party believes that a determined policy of separation between the European race and the non-European racial groups, and the application of the principle of separation between the non-European racial groups as well, is the only basis on which the character and the future of each race can be protected and made secure and enabled to develop in accordance with its own national character, abilities and destiny.

'In their own areas the non-European racial groups will be afforded a full opportunity of development and they will be able to develop their own institutions and social services, and in that way the abilities of the more progressive non-Europeans will be enlisted in the advancement of their own people.' …

What is the situation as it exists? Europeans and non-Europeans scattered and mingled about the whole South Africa; Europeans and non-Europeans travelling mixed in the trams and in the trains; Europeans and non-Europeans mixing are already in hotels and places where meals are served; engaged more and more in taking possession of the theatres and the streets; engaged in devastating the reserves; engaged in seeking learning which they do not use in the service of their own people, but which they use in order to try to cross the border line of European life, to become traitors to their own people and to desert their own people. That is the picture that one sees; that is the situation that one finds today; nobody can deny that. The public of South Africa are seeing it with their own eyes.

8 How were residential areas to be divided?

9 Why did the National Party believe it was important to separate the races?

10 What was the situation between the Europeans and non-Europeans at the time the speech was delivered?

BRINGING ORDER TO THE MANY APARTHEID LAWS

In this chapter, you have read about the many apartheid laws which tried to separate the races in South Africa.

- Which ones do you think had the greatest impact on the life of an average African?
- Use the chart below to make a list of the ten laws you think had the greatest impact on the people. Order these from most influential to least influential.
- Now share your ideas with a classmate. How does your order differ from your classmate's? What can explain the differences?

Apartheid laws with the greatest impact on the life of South Africans
1
2
3
4
5
6
7
8
9
10

Creation of townships and forced removals

■ Mixed areas

In the early twentieth century, growing numbers of Africans moved to urban areas in search of work. Some of them purchased land there and built homes. In a number of cities such as Johannesburg, Durban and Cape Town, entire neighbourhoods of people of different races lived side by side. Areas where sizeable numbers of Africans were landowners outside tribal reserves became known as 'black spots'. In 1923, the Native Urban Areas Act was passed. This banned different races from living in the same towns or neighbourhoods. Nonetheless, in some places people ignored the law.

■ Sophiatown

The most famous mixed-race location was Sophiatown, a suburb of Johannesburg. Its population grew dramatically during the Second World War when thousands of Africans migrated to the cities to work in the war industries. By 1950, 39,000 people were living in Sophiatown. While much of the town consisted of makeshift housing, it was a vibrant mixed community of Africans, Asians, coloureds and some white people, known for its lively music scene and nightlife.

Two new government laws put Sophiatown in the sights of the apartheid regime:

- The 1950 Group Areas Act meant that mixed neighbourhoods were forbidden. In the case of Sophiatown, that meant the people could be moved out and much of the area torn down.
- In 1954, the Native Resettlement Act permitted forced removals by the government of Africans living in and around Johannesburg to any location it deemed fit.

■ Reasons for the removal

One of the possible reasons for the decision to remove the Sophiatown inhabitants was that the permanent housing ran counter to the government's stated policy that Africans would only be allowed to live temporarily in proximity to white people. The permanent home of the Africans was, according to the government, the tribal homeland. African townships that grew up near cities often lacked plumbing and electricity. Workers often lived in barracks-like buildings, housing many workers. The townships, too, faced severe regulations. For example, they could not be built closer than half a kilometre to white suburbs.

■ Resistance to the removal

The Africans and the Indians did try to resist the government plans to forcibly remove the Sophiatown inhabitants. The ANC and the Transvaal Indian Congress (TIC) both organized demonstrations against the removal. Many of the Sophiatown residents took up the slogan, 'We Won't Move'. However, the authorities put on such massive displays of force that the ANC and the TIC realized that resistance would prove fruitless.

■ The end of Sophiatown

On 10 February 1953, two days before the announced date, 2000 policemen and many trucks arrived at Sophiatown. They quickly and ruthlessly removed hundreds of residents and their belongings on the first day and began to bulldoze homes. It would take another six years for the suburb to be emptied totally. Many of the inhabitants were moved to the new all-black township of Meadowlands. Sophiatown became an all-white suburb named Triomph or Triumph in 1962. It was meant to reflect the successful efforts to destroy this example of mixed-race living.

IDENTIFYING THE MAIN POINTS IN A SOURCE

- Question 13 of Paper 1 contains two parts, both of which test understanding of two different sources.
- Question 13b is a visual source. It can be a photograph, a cartoon, a chart or a map. Students are asked to identify the message of the source. List at least two messages from the source.
- Two or three sentences are enough to fulfil the demands of this question.

Examine Source E and then answer the question that follows it.

11 What does Source E suggest about the Sophiatown removals?

SOURCE E

Photograph taken by Terence Spencer in 1959 for *LIFE* magazine of the Sophiatown removals.

EXAMINING ORIGIN OF A SOURCE

- The second question of Paper 1 requires students to evaluate the value and limitations of a source based on its origin, purpose and content.
- The origin of a source comes from several components: author, title, date of origin, type of source, and, if applicable, title, publisher and type of publication. Information about origin can be found in the description of a source that precedes the source's text.
- The following questions are designed to make connections between the components of a source's origin and how they affect value or limitation.

Refer to Source F to answer the questions that follow the source. Use the topic: for a historian studying the Sophiatown removals.

SOURCE F

Extract from Trevor Huddleston, *Naught for Your Comfort*, 1956, quoted in John A. Williams, *From the South African Past: Narratives, Documents, and Debates*, Houghton Mifflin, Boston, 1997, pages 277–8. Huddleston was a white Church of England parish priest who served the people of Sophiatown.

… It was only when we got to Toby Street that we began to understand how things were shaping: that we knew for certain that the removal, so long talked about, so often and so fiercely debated, had actually begun. On the broad belt of grass between the European suburb of Westdene and Sophiatown … a whole fleet of lorries was drawn up: a grim sight against the grey, watery sky. Lining the whole street were thousands of police, both white and black: the former armed with rifles and revolvers, the latter with the usual assegai [spears]. A few Sten guns were in position at various points … 'Where are they beginning?' 'In the yard opposite the bus station, at the bottom of Toby Street … . Let's go.' It was a fantastic sight. It looked more like a film-set for an 'atmospheric' Italian film than anything real. In the yard, military lorries were drawn up. Already they were piled high with the pathetic possessions which had come from the row of rooms in the background. A rusty kitchen stove: a few blackened pots and pans: a wicker chair: mattresses belching out their coir-stuffing; bundles of heaven-knows-what, and people, soaked, all soaked to the skin by the drenching rain … .

The first lorries began to move off for Meadowlands eight miles [13 km] away to the west. The rain poured down. The removal was definitely under way. Two thousand police, armed; many foreign correspondents; dozens of photographers; a total ban on all gatherings, including (as we thought at the time) attendance at a church service. All this, to effect a slum-clearance scheme which would be of lasting benefit to the 'natives'; … . all this excitement and fuss and publicity over a project which to any sensible European in South Africa was a crying necessity if white civilization was to be preserved.

12 Who wrote the source?

13 When did he write this?

14 How is this source of value for a historian studying the Sophiatown removals?

15 What limitations does this source have for a historian studying the Sophiatown removals?

Segregation of education

■ School conditions

Before the 1948 National Party victory, the vast majority of Africans were taught in Church-run mission schools. These were subsidized by the government. However, only one-third of African children attended any sort of school and only a tiny percentage made it as far as high school. Schooling was not compulsory for Africans, unlike Europeans. Because of rapid urbanization and growing numbers of children, African schools were under pressure. Generally, they were overcrowded, underfunded and literally falling apart.

■ Werner Eiselen and his report

African schools were investigated soon after the new government took power. A commission was formed, led by the deputy secretary in the Department of Native Affairs, Werner Eiselen. From 1949 to 1951, the commission collected data and analysed reasons the school system for Africans was failing. The Eiselen Commission produced a 200-page report in 1949. Among its chief conclusions were:

- Education for Africans would best taught in the homelands.
- Education should be taught in tribal languages.
- Education should reflect the needs of the Africans; in other words, a western-style academic programme was not appropriate.
- Education should instil within Africans the ideas that they did not have equal rights and their development should be in their own sphere.
- African identity should be stressed and celebrated.

■ Bantu Education Act

Two years later, the government acted on the report and passed the Bantu Education Act of 1953. It called for:

- a transfer of control of African Education from the Ministry of Education to the Ministry of Native Affairs
- the removal of state subsidies for mission schools; consequently, most mission schools soon closed
- an increase in the role of the government in African education; the curriculum was also to be rewritten with a new focus on vocational training.

■ Impact of the Act

The Department of Native Affairs suddenly found itself in charge of 28,000 African teachers and many more responsibilities. Consequently, in 1955, a separate Department of Bantu Education was created.

All Churches in South Africa, with the exception of the Afrikaner Dutch Reformed Church, opposed the new legislation. The Churches were ordered to turn their schools over to the government by December 1954. Most Churches complied because they felt that forcing their students to leave school would be worse for their pupils. The number of Church-run schools dropped from 5000 in 1953 to only 589 in 1965. Meanwhile, the number of government schools increased from 230 to 7282 in the same time period.

The new Bantu curriculum stressed teaching students that their duties and responsibilities were to accept the natural domination of the white people. This was introduced at an early age. No longer would a student be able to study foreign languages or the sciences. Training to be a housemaid, a farm employee or a miner was considered to be the goal of Bantu education.

The ANC began a boycott of the new schools. The government responded by threatening to close down permanently any schools that participated in such a boycott. Parents chose to send their children to the new government schools, believing that even a bad education was preferable to no education at all. The boycott quickly fizzled out.

MAKING INFERENCES

- Often the reader needs to read between the lines to determine the significance of a given source.

Read the following source and answer the questions that follow.

SOURCE G

Extract from the 1953 Bantu Education Act, No. 47 (www.sahistory.org.za/archive/bantu-education-act%2C-act-no-47-of-1953).

Act. No. 47 of 1953

ACT. To provide for the transfer of the administration and control of native education from the several provincial administrations to the Government of the Union, and for matters incidental thereto.

Definitions. 1. In this Act, unless the context otherwise indicates—

(i) 'Bantu' shall be synonymous with 'native' …

(v) 'native' means any person who is or is generally accepted as a member of any aboriginal race or tribe of Africa …

Transfer of control … . 2. As from the date of commencement of this Act—

(a) the control of native education shall vest in the Government of the Union subject to the provisions of this Act;

(b) there shall cease to be vested in the executive committee in the executive of a province any powers, authorities and functions, and the provincial council of a province shall cease to be competent to make ordinances, in relation to native education: …

Administration. 3. (i) It shall be the function of the Department under the direction and control of the Minister [of Education], to perform all the work necessary for or incidental to the general administration of native education … .

16 What racial or ethnic groups are not discussed in this Act?
17 What political organization or authority would lose control over native education?
18 Who was the ultimate authority when it came to African education?

READING FOR CONTENT

- It is important to read the sources in Paper 1 closely, keeping in mind the questions which relate to them.
- In other words, be sure you address the demands of the question.

Read Source H closely and answer the questions that follow.

SOURCE H

Extract from Nelson Mandela's article 'Bantu Education Goes to University', published in *Liberation*, June 1957. Quoted in Nelson Mandela, *The Struggle is My Life*, Pathfinder Press, Atlanta, 1990, page 65.

He [Verwoerd] declared that racial relations could not improve if the wrong type of education was given to Africans. They could not improve if the result of African education was the creation of a frustrated people who, as a result of the education they received, had expectations in life which circumstances in South Africa did not allow to be fulfilled … . Above all, good racial relations could not exist when education was given under the control of people who believed in racial equality. It was therefore, necessary that African education should be controlled in such a way that it should be in accord with the policy of the State.

The Bantu Education Bill has now become law and it embodies all the obnoxious doctrines enunciated by the Minister in the parliamentary debate … An inferior type of education, known as Bantu education, and designed to relegate the Africans to a position of perpetual servitude in a baasskap society, is now in force in almost all African primary schools throughout the country and will be introduced in all secondary and high schools as from next year. The Separate Universities Education Bill, now before Parliament, is a step to extend Bantu education to the field of higher education.

19 What did Mandela believe were the true aims of Bantu education?
20 How was the government trying to change all levels of education in South Africa?

Bantustan system

Revised ☐

■ Creation of the Bantustans

As part of the policy to remove Africans from South Africa's political system, the government created an administrative mechanism known as the Bantustan system.

In 1951, the Bantu Authority Act was passed. This provided for the establishment of tribal homelands on the 13.5% of the land reserved for Africans, although they made up 70% of the population. It would take another act, the Promotion of Bantu Self-Government Act, in 1959, to put the finishing touches on exactly what the Bantustan system meant. Eight separate homelands were created. Each was meant to represent different tribal ethnic language groups. Africans would be grouped according to their language. The white government promoted this as 'separate development'.

The stated plans included the slow and steady development of the Bantustans into self-supporting and eventually independent nations. They were meant to be self-governing, even though the South African authorities were the ones who often appointed the chiefs in these homelands.

■ Reasons for the Bantustans

The reasons behind the government's actions were:

● To make Africans citizens of their homelands and not South Africa.
● To remove as many Africans as possible from South African urban areas.
● To remove Africans from the countryside when they were not needed. As agriculture became more mechanized, African labour was not needed all year. The government certainly did not want unemployed labourers near white farming areas so they were moved to the Bantustans.
● To deflect criticism from the growing nationalist movements on the continent. South Africans would proudly say that they were giving independence to their black people.

■ Life on the Bantustans

The impact and reality of the Bantustans did not live up to the lofty stated reasons. Africans suffered on the Bantustans because the conditions were often deplorable. What Africans often found were:

● No jobs. Unemployment was very high as up to 70% of the economically active population was forced into migrant labour outside the Bantustans. What little they earned in the mines and the farms was sent back to their families remaining in the tribal homelands.
● Only a small plot of land for each family. Bantustan land was usually the worst in South Africa, so the land did not produce enough to meet a family's needs. No grazing land was provided for livestock.
● No schools, shops, fuel or medical services. Additionally, they were often housed in tents.

The government forcibly relocated 3.5 million people from 1960 to 1982. The Bantustans served as dumping grounds for the unneeded and potentially unruly Africans.

■ Transkei

Transkei was the first Bantustan created, in 1963. It was supposed to be self-governing. It did have a parliament of sorts but many of the members were chosen, not elected. Transkei soon became essentially a one-party state, recognized internationally by only one country, South Africa. The Bantustan system was hated by the Africans and hailed by the whites. The reality was that they were miserable places with few opportunities. Internationally, they were seen as a hideous attempt by the government to paper over the horrors of apartheid.

COMPARING TWO SOURCES

- Question 15 asks you to compare and contrast two sources.
- Generally, this would mean locating three similarities and three differences in the two sources, although sometimes the split might be four to two.

Try to locate three similarities in the two sources below. Add a brief explanation on how they are similar. See a sample answer at the back of the book.

SOURCE I

Extract from W.J. de Kock, *History of South Africa*, Department of Information, Pretoria, 1971, pages 46–7. De Kock was a South African professor of History.

From 1949 onwards the Malan Government unhesitatingly introduced legislation to implement the policy of separate advancement of the race groups in South Africa; this was considered to be the only means by which cultural values in a multi-national country could be safeguarded and the only guarantee of racial peace because it provided an opportunity for development to the Non-White peoples … .

The man who determined the pattern of Bantu policy in the fifties was Dr. H.F. Verwoerd, who became Minister of Native Affairs in 1950 … . Verwoerd was dedicated to the task entrusted to him: he studied the Bantu in their homeland and in the teeming urban residential areas; Bantu history and its demands; Bantu tradition and its peculiarities; the Bantu mind and its workings. Verwoerd's study convinced him that the development of the Bantu should be based not on an extension of political rights in competition with the Whites, but on the traditional authority and order of their own national groups. This concept was embodied in the Bantu Authorities Act of 1951, which provided for the establishing of a hierarchy in the homelands … As Premier he continued to attach great importance to the realization of Bantu self-government, stressing the constructive aspects of the policy of separate independence for the Non-White peoples.

SOURCE J

Extract from Saul Dubow, *Apartheid 1948–1994*, Oxford University Press, Oxford, 2014, pages 63–4. Dubow is a professor of African History at the University of Cambridge. Dubow was born and raised in South Africa.

Within nationalist policy-making and political circles there was from the start a view that apartheid had to be presented as a morally defensible system which would be of advantage to all. This could only be sustained by insisting that the losses incurred by Africans in white urban areas would be made up by greater opportunities in the reserves. Christian National theory, *volks* nationalism, and cultural relativist ideas drawn from anthropological theory, all provided justification for the idea that cultures were unique systems that merited special treatment or protection. It followed that ethnic and national units should be accorded their own separate channels of expression and, perhaps, even a measure of political recognition.

This was the premise of the 1951 Bantu Authorities Act which provided for the creation of 'tribal authorities' in rural African reserves. It gave the government extensive powers to proclaim chiefs and councillors, regardless of whether they enjoyed popular legitimacy. Elements of direct and indirect rule were thereby built into a system of governance which, although centralized in Pretoria, was devolved to rural authorities at a local level. Although not apparent at the time, the Act laid the basis of the future Bantustans, notionally self-governing 'tribal' states whose emergence represented the apogee [highest point] of apartheid fantasy. The 1951 Act was bitterly opposed by Africans who rejected government-sponsored 'retribalization', viewing this as a further erosion of their residual citizenship rights.

Source booklet

Examine Source K below and answer question 16 in the accompanying question paper.

SOURCE K

'Non-white shop.' A photograph by Paul Weinberg taken in Kliptown, Johannesburg, 1979.

Sample question and answer

Below is a sample answer. Read it and the comments around it.

- Question 16 of Paper 1 requires a student to write an essay that incorporates the use of all four sources and your own knowledge in response to a specific question.
- In this case, 'your own knowledge' refers to relevant knowledge not found in the four sources.
- The question is worth 9 marks. It is the most valuable question and you should devote the most time to answering it.
- You should spend 20–25 minutes answering the question. It is recommended that the first five minutes be used to outline your response. You should spend the last twenty minutes writing the essay.
- In the question below, the command term 'analyse' means to ' break down in order to bring out the essential elements or structure' (*History Guide*, first examinations 2017, page 97). This requires students to identify important themes or factors that when put together explain the topic. Each of these themes or factors should be developed in separate paragraphs. All components should be linked back together in the conclusion.
- In order to answer the question you will need to use Sources F, G, J and K.

16 **Using these sources (F, G, J and K) and your own knowledge, analyse the impact of petty and grand apartheid on the African population.**

After coming to power in 1948, the National Party began to institute a new system of racial separation known as apartheid. The many apartheid laws which followed had an enormous impact on the African population as they reached into every aspect of the black people's lives. The laws affected the people economically, socially and politically. There were two different forms of apartheid laws, loosely categorized as grand and petty apartheid. Grand apartheid involved separating where people lived while petty apartheid meant the day-to-day restrictions such as separate facilities.

Clear introduction to the response.

In 1950, the South African Parliament passed two pieces of legislation which had major repercussions on the African population. The Group Areas Act gave the government the right to determine where people lived. Because the authorities were trying to separate the races to the greatest degree possible, this meant that many Africans were forced to move to their tribal areas or tribal reserves. These were often inhospitable and economically depressed areas that had been allocated to Africans by previous governments. As a consequence of the Act, more than one million people were moved to the reserves.

Another strategy that was part of this effort, were the forced removals. Here, the government deemed some urban areas in which different races lived side by side to be illegal. This was the case of Sophiatown, a thriving suburb of Johannesburg. As Source F clearly shows, the government used 2000 policemen to forcibly remove the people living in Sophiatown in 1955. Sophiatown was later razed to the ground in order to create an all-white neighbourhood. Africans could now only live in African-only areas, and coloureds in coloured-only neighbourhoods. Asians and whites were similarly affected. This grand apartheid legislation had torn up the social fabric of Sophiatown and was used on many occasions to enforce racial segregation.

The second piece of legislation which was also part of grand apartheid was the Bantu Authorities Act of 1951. Source J details how this created tribal authorities in the tribal reserves or homelands. The government was trying to force Africans to live on these reserves when their labour was needed on white farms or in factories. Supposedly, the tribal authorities would be self-governing even though, in reality, the government often chose the tribal chiefs. One consequence of the Bantu Authorities Act was that it tried to make the Africans citizens of their homelands and not of South Africa. It soon became clear that South Africa was to be reserved for white people only. People living in the homelands faced dire economic difficulties because there weren't many jobs available and there was little grazing land for animals. Many people lived on the little money that was sent from family members working in the mines or factories outside the homelands.

Petty apartheid had a huge impact on the daily lives of black people. In 1953, the Reservation of Separate Amenities Act was passed by parliament because segregation had not been universally applied throughout the country. This law meant that wherever and whenever possible the races were to be separated. Beaches and restaurants and post offices and toilets were segregated. As illustrated in Source K, even benches were restricted according to race. An African would be arrested if he chose to sit on the bench next to the children. Segregation notices appeared everywhere. Segregation that might have been customary was now legally enforced. In many regards, the social movement of Africans was becoming more and more restricted.

> Sources clearly referenced.

> Synthesis of own knowledge and sources.

5/9. The response would achieve the 4–6 mark band because while it is focused on the demands of the question, there is only explicit reference to three sources. The answer is also a bit unbalanced. More could have written about the impact of other petty apartheid laws such as the Bantu Education Act.

Exam practice

Now it's your turn to take a mock exam.

Read Sources M–P below and answer questions 13–16 in the accompanying question paper. The sources and questions relate to Case study 2: Apartheid South Africa 1948–64 – nature and characteristics of discrimination: segregation of education.

SOURCE M

A speech by the minister of native affairs, Dr Hendrik Verwoerd, to the Senate, 7 June 1954 (www. politicsweb.co.za/documents/hendrik-verwoerd-10-quotes).

It is the policy of my department that education should have its roots entirely in the Native areas and in the Native environment and Native community. There Bantu education must be able to give itself complete expression and there it will have to perform its real service. The Bantu must be guided to serve his own community in all respects. There is no place for him in the European community above the level of certain forms of labour. Within his own community, however, all doors are open.

For that reason it is of no avail for him to receive a training which has as its aim absorption in the European community while he cannot and will not be absorbed there. Up till now he has been subjected to a school system which drew him away from his own community and partically (sic) misled him by showing him the green pastures of the European but still did not allow him to graze there. This attitude is not only uneconomic because money is spent on education which has no specific aim, but it is even dishonest to continue with it. The effect on the Bantu community we find in the much discussed frustration of educated Natives who can find no employment which is acceptable to them. It is abundantly clear that unplanned education creates many problems, disrupts the communal life of the Bantu and endangers the communal life of the European.

For that reason it must be replaced by planned Bantu Education. In the Native territories where the services of educated Bantu are much needed, Bantu education can complete its full circle, by which the child is taken out of the community by the school, developed to his fullest extent in accordance with aptitude and ability and thereafter returned to the community to serve and to enrich it.

SOURCE N

An anti-Bantu education protest, 1955, photographed by a *Drum* magazine photographer. 'Baas' means 'master' or 'boss' and was supposed to be used when an African addressed a white. *Drum* was a South African magazine directed at Africans.

SOURCE O

Extract from Albert Luthuli, *Let My People Go: An Autobiography*, McGraw-Hill, New York, 1962, page 147. Chief Luthuli was one of the leaders of the ANC and a Nobel Peace Prize winner (1960).

We recognized fully – and the event has not proved us wrong – that the end of all true education for Africans was in sight, at least for the time being ... . The choice before parents is an almost impossible one – they do not want Bantu Education and they do not want their children on the streets. They have to choose between two evils, and no rule of thumb indicates which is the greater. The chances of universal agreement are small, not because of hesitation about whether Bantu Education is evil, but because, as Archbishop Clayton of Cape Town told his Synod, 'a rotten education' may be 'better than none'.

SOURCE P

Extract from Saul Dubow, *Apartheid 1948–1994*, Oxford University Press, Oxford, 2014, pages 55–6. Dubow is a professor of African History at the University of Cambridge. Dubow was born and raised in South Africa.

Perhaps the clearest signal of the government's intention to subordinate Africans was the Bantu Education Act of 1953. This measure aimed to bring all educational provision under the control of the state. It effectively meant the end of the independent church and mission school system which, for a century, had successfully schooled a small elite of Africans. Many mission school graduates had gone on to become political leaders. The intention of the Act was to suffocate independent thought and crush the aspirations of the improving elite ... .

Bantu education envisaged a system of enforced multiculturalism in which Africans would be schooled in a manner appropriate to their cultural development. Verwoerd's reference to pastures and grazing thus spoke to both constituencies: it likened Africans to simple docile animals, while also evoking the idea that blacks were naturally tribal and therefore best suited to life in the rural reserves where, in principle, there would be no constraint on their ambitions. Verwoerd's plans for Bantu education were calculated to appeal to the mass of ordinary Africans who remained outside the education system altogether.

13 a Why, according to Source M, was the Bantu Education Act needed? [3]
   b What does Source N suggest about the African reaction to the Bantu Education Act? [2]

14 With reference to its origin, purpose and content, analyse the value and limitations of Source O for a historian studying the impact of the Bantu Education Act. [4]

15 Compare and contrast what Sources M and P reveal about Minister Verwoerd's intentions. [6]

16 Using the sources and your own knowledge, evaluate the role the South African government played in African education in the 1950s. [9]

5 Protests and action

Defiance Campaign (1952–3)

▣ Non-violent protests

As the South African Parliament began to pass apartheid legislation, the South Africa Communist Party organized a one-day work stoppage and demonstrations on 1 May 1950. The police responded with force and eighteen Africans were killed. On 26 June, several groups, including the African National Congress (ANC), worked together to organize the National Day of Protest. While the event was not a success, the date 26 June became known as Freedom Day and would later be used to mark further significant events.

▣ ANC and South African Indian Congress (SAIC) work together

The ANC and the SAIC joined forces to combat the new apartheid laws that were harming the African and Asian communities. The Joint Planning Council met on 29 July 1951. At this meeting, the two groups decided to begin planning for a mass campaign to press for the repeal of a wide range of discriminatory laws. The laws targeted included:

- pass laws
- Group Areas Act
- Separate Representation of Voters Act
- Suppression of Communism Act
- Bantu Authorities Act.

On 21 January 1952, the ANC and SAIC sent letters to the prime minister calling for the repeal of the laws by 29 February. If this did not happen, a campaign of defiance would result. Malan responded that if the ANC continued to defy the authorities, it would be crushed. He ignored the SAIC.

▣ Defiance Campaign

The first of a series of demonstrations was held on 6 April. The ANC and SAIC met in Port Elizabeth on 27 April and planned to launch their campaign of defiance:

- The groups appealed for 10,000 volunteers.
- The campaign began on 26 June.
- All over the country, volunteers broke apartheid laws.
- They sat on benches and train compartments reserved for whites.
- They lined up at 'whites only' counters in post offices and railway stations.
- The courts soon filled up with the arrested volunteers.
- Between June and December 1952, 8557 had been arrested by the authorities.
- The South African and international press covered the campaign extensively, embarrassing the government.
- Even the United Nations (UN) took notice and set up a commission of inquiry to visit South Africa.
- The South African government did not allow the commission entry into the country.

In January 1953, the ANC called off the campaign. Because it was mostly located in the East Cape, it did not engage Africans throughout the country and, so, lost some of its initial energy. There were also fears that rioting was getting out of control and becoming too violent, thereby confirming the government's warnings about the campaign. Still, the Defiance Campaign had:

- created a mass-scale movement as ANC membership exploded from 5000 to 100,000 members
- challenged racial discrimination and united the ANC and the SAIC in a common cause
- stressed non-violence and was able to keep most of its members in line, even though they were often provoked by the authorities

- made the horrors of apartheid known globally
- raised the consciousness of non-whites and whites alike; in fact, some whites supported the goals of the campaign.

However, not one apartheid law was repealed. The government passed even more laws to crush disobedience. These included the 1953 Criminal Law Amendment Act and the Public Safety Act. The Criminal Law Amendment Act stated that acts of civil disobedience could be punishable with jail terms up to five years, heavy fines and whippings 'not exceeding ten lashes'. The Public Safety Act allowed the government to institute a state of emergency anywhere in the country. In such cases, the police would have the right to act in any way they determined best.

EXAMINING CONTENT OF A SOURCE

- Content refers to the information contained in a source.
- Content value comes from information in the source that supports the topic being studied.
- Content limitation comes from information in the source that does not match the topic being examined or information found in the source that addresses only part of the scope of the topic being examined.

For the questions below, refer to Source A below. The questions are designed to make connections between the source's content and how it affects the value and limitation. Use the topic: for a historian studying the Defiance Campaign.

SOURCE A

Extract from an article 'South Africa Tries Race Ban Defiers' in the *New York Times*, 27 August 1952.

Twenty top leaders of the growing passive resistance campaign against the Government's apartheid, or racial segregation, laws faced a court here today on charges of encouraging communism while 2,000 supporters outside the building roared, booed and chanted the national anthem …

Today's hearing started a preliminary examination to determine whether the twenty African and Indian Congress leaders could be tried under the country's Suppression of Communism Act. The prosecution charged the defendants with 'encouraging achievement of the objects of communism' by the resistance campaign …

The twenty accused, many wearing the black, green and yellow colors of the African National Congress, filled the large dock and overflowed onto long benches …

Meanwhile, mass arrests took place in Port Elizabeth, Cape Town, and Roodepoort, near Johannesburg, in a new wave of defiance to the 'unjust racial laws'. …

A total of 426 persons across the country were arrested for ignoring 'European only' signs in railroad stations and in other public places.

This is the highest daily total since the passive resistance campaign started two months ago. Most were Africans though some were various East Indian races.

1 What evidence is there in Source A that the Defiance Campaign is a large protest movement?
2 How is the article's content valuable for a historian studying the Defiance Campaign?
3 What are the limitations of the content?

Freedom Charter (1955)

Proposed Congress of the People

After the Defiance Campaign, the ANC and its allies, hoping to keep up momentum, called for a nationwide meeting. At the proposed Congress of the People were to be representatives from trade unions, women's groups, the ANC, Indian Congress, Coloured People's Organisation and the Congress of Democrats, most of whom were white members of the banned Communist Party.

ANC volunteers spread across the country to ask citizens from different ethnic and social backgrounds what they wanted in a new South Africa. The many responses were catalogued and organized so they could be voted on later and incorporated into a final document.

The Congress of the People

The Congress met at Kliptown outside Johannesburg from 25 to 26 June 1955. While many of the leaders of the various groups attending had been under banning orders which forbade free movement of travel, some like Nelson Mandela and Walter Sisulu of the ANC watched the proceedings in secret. Almost 3000 delegates gathered in what was the most racially and economically diverse gathering in South Africa's history. There were 320 Indians, 230 Coloureds, 112 white people and 2200 Africans. They had braved police harassment to attend the historic meeting. Not all the delegates were in complete agreement. Some felt that the current situation of the black Africans should be the focus of any future South Africa while others argued for an all-inclusive coalition for every racial group. In the end, the latter viewpoint was the one adopted.

The Freedom Charter

The final document produced by the Congress of the People was the Freedom Charter. Each clause was voted on by the assembled delegates. Among the chief provisos of the Freedom Charter were:

- one person, one vote
- all national groups shall have equal rights
- all people shall share in the nation's wealth
- all shall be equal before the law
- all shall enjoy human rights
- trade unions shall be recognized and there shall be equal pay for equal work
- education shall be free, compulsory and equal for all children
- there shall be housing, security and free medical care.

This document served as the programme for the anti-apartheid movement for the next 40 years.

The government response

In December 1956, the government arrested 156 people who represented nearly 50 organizations that had been associated with the Congress of the People. These included a mix of 105 Africans, 23 whites, 21 Indians and seven Coloureds. The arrested included Nelson Mandela and almost every other significant anti-apartheid leader. They were all charged with high treason because it was claimed that the Freedom Charter was essentially a communist-inspired document. The court case, known as the Treason Trial, lasted from 1956 to 1961 and had several phases. During the first one, most of those charged had their indictments dropped. In the final phase, the remaining 30 defendants, all members of the ANC, were found not guilty, and the ANC was declared to be non-violent and not a communist-front organization.

INTERPRETING A PHOTOGRAPHIC SOURCE

- Question 13b will refer to a visual source.
- This will often be a photograph.
- You should try to come up with at least two possible items in your answer.

Examine the photo below closely and then answer the question that follows.

SOURCE B

This photograph was taken in 1956 by Eli Weinberg, a Latvian who lived in South Africa for decades but never took South African citizenship. He had been a member of the South African Communist Party and an active trade unionist. Because of the sheer number of those accused, Weinberg took five photographs and put these together into one photomontage.

4   What does Source B suggest about those accused of treason in 1956?

Alexandra Bus Boycott (January to June 1957)

■ Alexandra Bus Boycott

In January 1957, the Public Utility Transport Corporation (PUTCO) raised fares by 25% or one penny. For the tens of thousands of poor Africans who commuted daily from Alexandra to their work in Johannesburg, this was intolerable given their extremely low wages. The bus riders decided to boycott the buses until the fare was reduced to its former level:

- Within days, up to 70,000 boycotted the buses.
- They took up the slogan *Azikhwelwa!* (Zulu for 'We will not ride!') and were organized by the newly formed Alexandra People's Transport Action Committee (APTAC).
- Soon, sympathetic riders elsewhere joined in the boycott even though their fares had not increased.
- The distance between Alexandra and Johannesburg was roughly 10 miles (16 km) and most people had to walk this to reach their work.
- In some cases, sympathetic whites offered the boycotters rides, or if the boycotter was fortunate enough to own a bicycle, he or she could cycle to Johannesburg.

■ Government response

When the strike began, the minister of transport said the government would not 'give way, no matter whether the boycott lasts a month or six months'. He and others in the government felt the boycott was politically motivated rather than due to economic necessity.

The police responded to the mass action by threatening people, stopping and searching them, detaining them and deflating their bicycle tyres. Some workers were too tired to make the long walk home, so they slept in workers' hostels. These were raided nightly and Alexandra residents were arrested because they did not have permission to spend the night away from their designated area. They also harassed any white drivers who transported the boycotters to and from Johannesburg. During the course of the boycott, the police arrested 14,000 black people for 'document' violations.

The government finally surrendered in June 1957 under pressure from companies that did not always have a reliable source of workers because of the boycott. Employers and the city council agreed to contribute funds to cover the fare increase.

■ Significance of the boycott

The bus boycott was significant because:

- it demonstrated the potential strength of unified action
- it was one of the few non-violent methods open to people suffering under apartheid
- it showed that protests could be successful.

■ The Potato Boycott

After the success of the bus boycott, other protests followed. Terrible working conditions existed on farms that used the labour of unemployed Africans and prisoners. Often, they were given nothing besides a bit of food and rough shelter. On some farms, the adult and child workers had to dig up potatoes with their bare hands. A boycott of potatoes began in 1957, directed by the ANC, and many people soon refused to purchase them after learning of the dire conditions on the farms. The potatoes quickly rotted. In 1959, the farmers began to improve working conditions.

SUMMARIZE THE ARGUMENTS

- Question 16 asks you to use sources and your own knowledge to answer a specific question.
- In order to do this, you need to quickly determine the argument in each source.

Read Source C closely and then answer the question that follows. In order to do this, you need to quickly determine the argument in each source and you can use the table below to list four key points.

SOURCE C

Extract from Ruth First's article 'The Bus Boycott' in *Africa South*, Vol. 1.4, July–September 1957. It was later included in M.J. Daymond and C. Sandwith, *Africa South: Viewpoints, 1956–1961*, University of KwaZulu-Natal Press, Scottsville, 2011, pages 87–8. First was a committed activist who wrote this piece while facing charges in the Treason Trial. First later fled South Africa and was assassinated by South African security forces.

The government alarm at the bus boycott sprang from its pathological fear of allowing the African giant to feel – and use – his strength.

Nine years of Nationalist rule have been spent trying to bind the limbs of this giant, to halter and cripple him, to blindfold and muzzle him. The only answer to African demands that the Nationalists know is the threat, the restriction, the prohibition, the ban, the deportation order, the baton and the bullet … .

Above all, the bus boycott highlights other lessons for South Africans. It often takes such dramatic episodes to convince complacent white South Africa that Africans feel their denial of rights so keenly. And it showed Africans what they had suspected and now know for certain: that in active campaigning for basic human and economic demands, their unity holds the key to success.

5   What are the key points raised in this source?

Key point 1	
Key point 2	
Key point 3	
Key point 4	

Sharpeville Massacre (1960)

▨ Pan Africanist Congress (PAC)

Not all Africans believed in the ANC strategy of seeking negotiations with the government or with its multiracial approach. In April 1959, the Pan Africanist Congress (PAC) was formed. It believed itself to be part of the larger movement sweeping through Africa, a movement that was trying to rid the continent of colonialism. The PAC also took advantage of the fact that much of the ANC leadership had been arrested as part of the Treason Trial. The charismatic Robert Sobukwe became the head of PAC and directed many of its activities.

▪ PAC–ANC rivalry

The ANC had declared that on 31 March 1960, there would be large-scale protests against the hated pass laws. The PAC hoped to increase its own visibility and steal some of the ANC's popularity by announcing its own series of demonstrations called for on 21 March.

Most of the demonstrations organized by the PAC were small scale and did not bring much attention. One exception was in Sharpeville, about twelve miles (20 km) from Johannesburg.

▨ Sharpeville

Sharpeville was a community of about 37,000 Africans. It suffered from high unemployment, particularly among the young. There was also acute resentment because local factories relied on cheaper imported migrant labour instead of those whose homes were in Sharpeville. It was in this volatile mix that the PAC was able to radicalize young people.

In 1959, a new police station was built. The officers were very active in checking passes, deporting illegal residents and busting up beer dens. In other words, the community was at odds with the authorities much of the time.

▪ Sharpeville Massacre

As the demonstration began on 21 March 1960, up to 20,000 people gathered to protest the pass laws. The plan was to go to the police station and show the policemen that they had no passes. Then, they would demand to be arrested. The police did not have the means to process so many people. However, as the crowd moved closer to the police state, it appears that a policeman was pushed over by the crowd. Panicked policemen opened fire on the protesters. In minutes, 69 were dead and almost 200 wounded. An investigation found that 70% of those killed had been shot in the back, meaning that they were running away from the police, not towards them.

Contributing factors to the violence:

- The police were on edge after several other policemen had been killed in riots elsewhere.
- There was indecisive police leadership at Sharpeville.
- The day was very hot and tempers rose.
- A PAC leader had been arrested shortly before the police opened fire; some believed he might have been able to keep the demonstrators' anger in check.

▪ Government response

The massacre was widely reported and quickly condemned by the UN Security Council and many foreign governments. Prime Minister Hendrik Verwoerd, on the other hand, praised the police forces. In Sharpeville, the police went into the hospital and arrested some of the wounded. PAC leaders were seized and severely beaten in cells. The police even went so far as to plant rocks and other weapons in the hands of the dead to demonstrate how the protesters were armed. In the rest of South Africa, the situation rapidly deteriorated.

▪ Langa violence

Also on 21 March, thousands of protesters had gathered at Langa township, a suburb of Cape Town, and were led by PAC activist Philip Kgosana. The plan was the same as at Sharpeville. The protesters were to march to the police station to turn themselves in for arrest. However, at the last minute, the march was cancelled and people dispersed. That evening, some protesters regrouped but were met by police who opened fire and killed three unarmed protesters and wounded many others.

COMPARING AND CONTRASTING TWO SOURCES

● Question 15 will ask you to compare and contrast two sources.

Read the following two sources and make a list of three similarities and three differences.

SOURCE D

Extract from Bernardus Fourie's statement to the UN during the special session of the Security Council meeting to discuss Sharpeville. Published in *Africa Today*, Vol. 7, No. 3, May 1960, page 6. Fourie was South Africa's ambassador to the UN.

… By intimidation of and threats to persons who do not belong to the group, the extremists managed to gather a crowd of approximately 20,000 people in a township, Sharpeville, in the Transvaal and a crowd of about 6,000 at Langa in the Cape Province. Police were in the areas concerned to exercise normal control, if needed, as is done in all well-ordered societies all over the world when large masses of demonstrators gather. At Sharpeville, some agitators immediately adopted a threatening attitude towards the police. Attempts were made to arrest some of the violators, but the crowd became more belligerent and the police were attacked with a variety of weapons: pangs, axes, iron-bars, knives, stick and firearms. Indeed, shots were fired at the police before the police returned fire in order to defend their own lives and also to forestall what might have led to even greater and more tragic bloodshed. I need hardly say how deeply the Union Government regrets that there was this tragic loss of life. The action that the police were forced to take must be seen against a background not known to many people outside South Africa. Not two months before the latest tragedy, a group of nine policemen was brutally battered to death by a so-called 'unarmed', peace group … .

While it is easy, when 10,000 miles removed, to criticize the authorities for having used firearms on this occasion, it is indeed asking too much of a small group of policemen to commit suicide, to stand by idly awaiting their turn to be stoned to death. … No Government can allow hundreds of thousands of its citizens to be intimidated by extremists, as the Bantu in South Africa often are …

SOURCE E

Extract from an article by Humphrey Tyler, the white editor of *Drum* magazine. Tyler was one of two journalist witnesses. Published in *Africa Today*, Vol. 7, No. 3, May 1960, page 5.

The crowd seemed to be loosely gathered around the Saracens [armoured tanks] and on the fringes people were walking in and out. The kids were playing. In all there were about 3,000 people. They seemed amiable. Suddenly there was a sharp report from the direction of the police station. There were shrill cries of 'Izwe Lethu' (our land) – women's voices, I thought. The cries came from the police station and I could see a small section of the crowd swirl around the Saracens. Hands went up in the Africanist salute. Then the shooting started. We heard the chatter of a machine-gun, then another, then another …

Hundreds of kids were running, too. One little boy had on an old black coat, which he held up behind his head, thinking, perhaps, that it might save him from the bullets. Some of the children, hardly as tall as the grass, were leaping like rabbits. Some were shot, too. Still the shooting went on. One of the policemen was standing on top of a Saracen, and it looked as though he was firing his Sten gun into the crowd …

Before the shooting, I heard no warning to the crowd to disperse. There was no warning volley. When the shooting started it did not stop until there was no living thing on the huge compound in front of the police station. The police have claimed they were in desperate danger because the crowd was stoning them. Yet only three policemen were reported to have been hit by stones – and more than 200 Africans were shot down. The police also have said that the crowd was armed with 'ferocious weapons' which littered the compound after they fled. I saw no weapons, although I looked very carefully, and afterwards studied the photographs of the death scene. While I was there I saw only shoes, hats and a few bicycles left among the bodies.

6   Create a list of at least three similarities and three differences found in the two sources.

■ The aftermath of Sharpeville

■ Langa march

In response to Sharpeville, Chief Luthuli of the ANC called for a national day of mourning on 28 March. For the first time in South African history, a national strike took place. Hundreds of thousands of workers stayed at home.

Serious disturbances erupted throughout South Africa after the Sharpeville and Langa killings. A group of 30,000 peaceful protesters marched from the township of Langa to the city centre of Cape Town on 31 March. They were led by PAC leader Philip Kgosana. This was an unprecedented demonstration right in the heart of the parliamentary capital of the country. Kgosana was persuaded to call off the march because he was promised a meeting with the justice minister. Kgosana feared police violence so he agreed to dismiss the protesters. They duly left Cape Town. Kgosana never did get to meet the justice minister because he was arrested after the marchers had departed. The police then moved into Langa where they beat and arrested scores of people who had participated in the march.

■ Effects of Sharpeville

The Sharpeville Massacre had many short- and long-term effects. These included:

- The economy was hurt. Foreign investors pulled money out of the country.
- 2000 political leaders were arrested.
- A state of emergency was declared. The army reserves were mobilized to help put down any disturbances. Public meetings were banned.
- An international outcry. The actions of the South African police were condemned across the globe.
- White emigration surpassed white immigration. White people became more fearful and began to arm themselves in increasing numbers.
- Some Afrikaner politicians began to question apartheid policies as being too heavy-handed.
- The ANC and PAC were banned under the new Unlawful Organizations Act of 7 April 1960.

■ Attempted assassination of Verwoerd

In the midst of this crisis, Prime Minister Verwoerd was shot in an attempted assassination. His temporary successor, Paul Sauer, created intense discussion when he suggested that a new approach was needed in light of the Sharpeville Massacre. However, from his hospital bed, Verwoerd sent word that the government would be even harsher in applying apartheid laws.

■ Government crackdown

The government arrested 18,000 people, mostly Africans. Under harsh police measures, the opponents were beaten into submission. The last chance of peaceful protests had ended.

■ South Africa becomes a republic

Verwoerd decided to press his case by calling for a referendum on 5 October 1960. White voters were asked to choose whether or not they wished South Africa to become a republic, thereby dropping their formal ties to Britain. By a narrow margin, the voters agreed to South Africa becoming a republic. Verwoerd then petitioned the British Commonwealth for South Africa to remain in the organization but as a republic. Many other members in the Commonwealth, such as India, Ghana and Canada, were highly critical of South Africa's racial policies and it was quite possible that they would force South Africa to leave the group. Before that could happen, Verwoerd withdrew South Africa from the Commonwealth on 31 May 1961, with South Africa becoming a republic with no ties to Britain.

COMBINING INFORMATION FROM A SOURCE AND OUTSIDE KNOWLEDGE

- Question 16 will ask you to use sources and own knowledge in order to answer a specific question.
- Own knowledge means any knowledge or understanding of a topic not found in the sources provided in the exam booklet.

Read the following source and then answer the question. You should read the previous page and add relevant information to expand on your use of the source.

SOURCE F

Extract from the Unlawful Organizations Act, 7 April 1960 (www.sahistory.org.za/archive/ unlawful-organizations-act%2C-act-no-34-of-1960).

Be it enacted by the Queen's Most Excellent Majesty, the Senate and the House of Assembly of the Union of South Africa, as follows:—

1. (1) If the Governor-General is satisfied that the safety of the public or the maintenance of public order is seriously threatened or is likely to be seriously threatened in consequence of the activities of the body knows as the Pan Africanist Congress or the body known as the African National Congress, he may, without notice of the body concerned, by proclamation in the Gazette declare such body, including all branches, sections or committees thereof, and all local, regional or subsidiary bodies forming part thereof, to be an unlawful organization.

7 Using the source and your own knowledge, explain why and how the government cracked down on the Pan Africanist Congress and the African National Congress.

Decision to adopt armed struggle

Revised ▢

▣ Ineffectiveness of non-violence

After the deaths at Sharpeville, a renewed focus on mass action was undertaken by the ANC. Many people burned their pass books and the sheer size of this lawlessness prompted the government to suspend temporarily the law requiring the carrying of the hated document. But this seeming victory was short lived. The government then said that Africans could no longer collect their pensions without a pass book:

- From 25 to 26 March, an All-in-Africa conference was held in Pietermaritzburg.
- About 1400 delegates representing 145 religious, political and cultural groups gathered.
- The government ignored their call for an end to apartheid.

It became increasing clear to the leadership of the ANC that the enormous expenditure of energy, time and money trying to end apartheid was a failure. The leadership, now meeting in secret because the ANC had been declared an illegal organization, began to think of alternative responses to the racist policies of the government.

▣ Discussions on the formation of an armed ANC wing

While it is unclear as to who first proposed the establishment of a military branch of the ANC, Nelson Mandela was certainly involved. At a secret meeting of the ANC, Mandela suggested that the ANC should sponsor an armed wing. One obstacle to this was Chief Luthuli, who was an ardent proponent of non-violence. Luthuli later suggested that the military branch should be a separate entity but under the control of the ANC leadership. The reasoning behind this was to make sure that the ANC allies who had not been outlawed, such as the Indian Congress and the Coloured People's Organisation, would not be charged once violence did break out.

▣ The creation of *Umkhonto we Sizwe*

Nelson Mandela and Joe Slovo of the South African Communist Party were given the task of creating the armed branch. The new group was named *Umkhonto we Sizwe*, which meant Spear of the Nation in both Zulu and Xhosa. It was often referred to as MK.

The MK planned to first carry out sabotage against government installations before moving on to guerrilla warfare. Every effort was made to spare civilian casualties.

On 16 December 1961, MK carried out its first acts of sabotage. It chose 16 December because that was the date of the annual South African holiday which commemorated the Afrikaner victory over the Zulu in 1838 at Blood River. Ten small explosive devices went off in Johannesburg and Port Elizabeth.

▣ *Poqo*

The PAC had also formed a military wing. It was called *Poqo*, meaning pure. Unlike the MK, *Poqo* hoped to inflict maximum violence on those it considered to be enemies of a free South Africa. The group targeted Langa policemen, government informers and the chiefs of the Transkei homeland, who were seen as government collaborators.

▣ The government response

In the first eighteen months of armed struggle, the two groups carried out approximately 200 missions. Little significant damage was done and white people did not become more fearful because the attacks were so small. The government response was quick and fierce, though. Among the measures it took were as follows:

- The Sabotage Act of 1962. Those charged with acts of sabotage faced the death penalty. One was presumed guilty until found innocent. Security forces now had a free hand to torture prisoners.
- General Laws Amendment Act of 1963. The authorities could arrest anyone for 90 days without charging them with crimes. Once the 90 initial days had passed, they could charge them and then hold the same person for another 90 days. This could continue indefinitely.
- Bantu Laws Amendment Act of 1964. The authorities could deport any African from any urban or farming area for any reason.

EXAMINING A SOURCE'S PURPOSE

- Question 14 of Paper 1 requires students to evaluate the value and limitations of a source based on its origin, purpose and content.
- The purpose of a source refers to why the author created the source.
- Knowing why a source was created can provide some insight into what kind of information was included and what kind of information may have been omitted.
- It also may give an indication to the perspective of the author.

Answer the question that follows Source G. Source G refers to the ANC's decision to adopt armed struggle.

SOURCE G

Extract from a speech by Nelson Mandela which appears in his *The Struggle is My Life*, Pathfinder Press, Atlanta, 1990, page 162. At the Rivonia Trial (see page 100), Mandela gave a four-hour speech during his trial in 1963. He explained his role in the creation of MK, among other issues.

I have already mentioned that I was one of the persons who helped to form Umkhonto. I, and the others who started the organization, did so for two reasons. Firstly, we believed that as a result of government policy, violence by the African people had become inevitable, and that unless responsible leadership was given to canalize and control the feelings of our people, there would be outbreaks of terrorism which would produce an intensity of bitterness and hostility between the various races of this country which is not produced even by war. Secondly, we felt that without violence there would be no way open to the African people to succeed in their struggle against the principle of white supremacy. All lawful modes of expressing opposition to this principle had been closed by legislation and we were placed in a position in which we had either to accept a permanent state of inferiority, or to defy the government. We chose to defy the law. We first broke the law in a way which avoided any recourse to violence; when this form was legislated against, and then the government resorted to a show of force to crush opposition to its policies, only then did we decide to answer violence with violence.

8   How might the fact that Mandela was the author of the speech affect its value as a historical source?

Rivonia Trial (1963–4)

◼ Mandela outside South Africa

After Nelson Mandela and the other accused were found not guilty at the Treason Trial and freed, he went underground because the ANC had been outlawed. In 1962, he secretly left South Africa and went to several African countries to raise support for what he hoped would be a South African guerrilla force. In Ethiopia, he addressed the Pan-African Freedom Conference. His speech outlining the difficult days to come in trying to overthrow apartheid was warmly received by the delegates, many of whom came from countries that either had recently become independent or were in the midst of anti-colonial wars.

◼ Mandela on trial again

For seventeen months, Mandela went into hiding, or underground. On his return to South Africa, the authorities captured him and put him on trial for incitement to violence and for leaving the country without a passport. On 7 November, he was found guilty on both counts and sentenced to five years with hard labour. As he left the court, he repeated the cry *Amandla!* (Power!) and the large crowd of his supporters responded with *Ngawethu!* (To us!) or *Power to the People!* Mandela was soon sent to the maximum security prison on Robben Island near Cape Town to serve his term in solitary confinement.

◼ Government raid on Liliesleaf Farm

The sabotage campaign continued, as did the government crackdown. On 12 July 1963, the security forces raided Liliesleaf Farm in the Johannesburg district of Rivonia. They seized seventeen MK members, weapons and incriminating documents. Mandela's role in the armed resistance was clearly stated in the documents.

◼ Charges against MK members

Mandela was taken from Robben Island and put in a Pretoria prison. He and nine others were charged with the following:

- recruiting people to train to use explosives
- conspiring to commit acts of sabotage and to aid foreign military units when they invaded South Africa
- acting to further communist objectives
- getting money from sympathizers abroad to carry out these plans.

Among the other defendants were important MK leaders such as Walter Sisulu and Govan Mbeki. There were also several white people and Indians who faced the death penalty for their 'crimes'.

◼ Rivonia Trial

The trial opened on 9 October 1963 at the Palace of Justice in Pretoria. It would last until 12 June 1964. Mandela was 'Accused No. 1'. He pleaded not guilty, as did his co-defendants. Even though the government presented damning evidence, the defence put up a spirited argument. When, on 20 April, Mandela spoke to the court, his supporters, and members of the local and foreign press, he turned the charges against him into an indictment against apartheid. He spoke for four hours. His speech is considered by many to be among the greatest of the twentieth century. He ended the speech declaring, 'I have cherished the ideal of a democratic and free society in which all persons live together in harmony and with equal opportunities. It is an ideal which I hope to live for and to achieve. But if needs be, it is an ideal for which I am prepared to die.'

The judge, Quartus de Wet, took three weeks to reach a verdict. Although the prosecutor had been pressing for the death penalty, the judge sentenced eight of the defendants to life in prison. Denis Goldberg, the lone white person found guilty, spent 22 years in a Pretoria prison. It remains unclear what motivated the judge to avoid the death penalty but there was a great deal of international agitation for clemency. Mandela was sent back to Robben Island with six of the other defendants. He would spend the next 27 years there.

MIND MAP

- The Rivonia Trial may be the topic of a Paper 1 exam.
- Even if it is not a specific topic, the many connections that can be made to the trial make it potentially useful as own knowledge for the last question of a Paper 1 exam requiring students to use all the sources and their own knowledge.

Use the information from the opposite page and from Source H to add details to the mind map below.

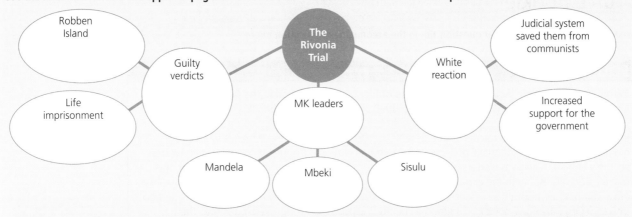

SOURCE H

Extract from Kenneth Broun, *Saving Nelson Mandela: The Rivonia Trial and the Fate of South Africa*, Oxford University Press, New York, 2012, pages 137–8. Broun is a professor emeritus of Law at the University of North Carolina School of Law.

The South African government had won the battle of Rivonia in many respects. The most effective and prominent of the black leaders, Mandela and Sisulu, were now safely out of the way for the rest of their lives. And indeed there would be no serious threat of civil unrest until the Soweto Uprising of June 16, 1976, which was led by an entirely new generation of activists … After the Rivonia Trial the government had won over white public opinion within South Africa and had driven black resistance deep underground. Most white South Africans were convinced that the police and the judicial system had saved them from a Communist-inspired revolution. While some seeds of concern had been planted – as illustrated by the *Rand Daily Mail* and *Pretoria News* editorials – among more moderate whites, the majority were unwavering in their support of the government.

To some extent that victory extended overseas as well. The life sentences and acquittals of James Kantor and Lionel Bernstein had convinced some … that South Africa's courts had operated fairly and independently. Still, most knowledgeable people abroad realized that no matter how independent the judiciary was, it was enforcing apartheid. And more importantly in the long run, the international publicity had created heroes, living heroes …

COMPARING AND CONTRASTING TWO SOURCES

- Question 15 will ask you to compare and contrast two sources.

Read Sources H and I closely and then answer the questions below.

SOURCE I

Extract from Thomas Karis and Gail M. Gerhart, *From Protest to Challenge. A Documentary History of South African Politics in South Africa, 1882–1964*, Vol. 3, *Challenge and Violence, 1953–1964*, Hoover Institution Press, Stanford, 1977, page 684. The late Thomas Karis was a professor at City University in New York. Gail Gerhart is a professor at Columbia University. Both authors have written extensively on South African history.

The ending of the Rivonia trial did not appear to stir white public opinion. The press praised the police, the prosecutor, and the judge, and evidence of effective security contributed to growing white complacency and support for the government. Within a week of the sentencing, four incidents of sabotage were reported, probably the work of the mainly white African Resistance Movement. Within a month or so, the police had smashed this idealistic and heroic but ineffectual group …

White South Africa, confident that it faced no dangerous challenge from the United States or other Western states, was facing a period in which white strength was to be consolidated rather than undermined and white initiatives to enlist black collaboration and compliance were to be accelerated. Meanwhile, Lutuli's bitter verdict on Rivonia stood: sentencing 'brave just men … to he shut away for long years in the brutal and degrading prisons of South Africa … will leave a vacuum in leadership', he said. 'With them will be interred this country's hopes for racial co-operation.'

9 What are two similarities found in Sources H and I?   10 What are two differences found in Sources H and I?

Exam focus

Source booklet

Read Source J below and answer question 13a in the accompanying question paper.

SOURCE J

Extract from an article 'South Africa on the Eve of Elections', published in the Royal Institute of International Affairs' *The World Today*, **Vol. 9, No. 2, February 1953, page 70.**

But the Africans are by no means united behind the Defiance Campaign, which is sponsored mainly by the African National Congress and the Indian National Congress. Many African leaders strongly criticize Congress leaders. Some do so because they disagree with the association of former Communists with the campaign. Others believe that it is 'reckless adventurism' to launch a mass campaign without first having organized mass support. A relatively new body, the Federation of Bantu Organizations, attacks Congress as being irresponsible. Congress alleges that the Federation is the tool of the Nationalist Government. The fact that Nationalist Ministers warmly commend the Federation lends some point to this accusation.

Despite these deep divisions between the non-Whites, the African National Congress has emerged as the most influential organization of Africans in the Union. This is mainly due to the success of the Defiance Campaign, its militancy, and the skill shown by its leaders – many of whom are now either in prison or have had their political rights circumscribed under the Law for the Suppression of Communism.

Sample questions and answers

Below is a sample answer. Read it and the comments around it.

- Question 13 of Paper 1 contains two parts, both of which test understanding of two different sources.
- Question 13a always refers to a narrative excerpt. Students are asked to identify main points from the source. This part of the question is worth 3 marks. That means three main points must be identified. Do not go into too much detail. List at least three main points. **Note:** the phrase 'main points' means important understandings from the source. It **does not** mean simply listing facts from the source.
- The two parts of question 13 should take about five minutes to answer.

13a According to Source J, why did some Africans not support the ANC?

> There are several reasons why not all Africans supported the ANC. First, a number of leaders felt that the ANC's Defiance Campaign had ties to former communists. Also, others believed that a mass campaign that had not first enlisted mass support was doomed to failure.

2/3. The response includes two good points. However, three points are needed to score 3 marks. A fuller response would have included: The Federation of Bantu Organizations did not support the ANC because it believed the ANC was 'irresponsible'.

Source booklet

Look at Source K closely and answer question 13b in the accompanying question paper.

SOURCE K

An estimated 30,000 protesters march from Langa into Cape Town to demand the release of prisoners held at the police station in Caledon Square, 31 March 1960.

Sample questions and answers

Below is a sample answer. Read it and the comments below it.

- Question 13 of Paper 1 contains two parts, both of which test understanding of two different sources.
- Question 13b is always a non-text source, that is, a political cartoon, propaganda poster, photograph, map or graph.
- Students are asked to identify two main messages or points from the source. The maximum value for 13b is 2 points. Students are asked to identify two main points from the source.
- Try to have at least 2 specific points in your answer. If you have made 3 points and one is incorrect, you will still score full (2) marks.

13b   What does Source K suggest about the 1960 Langa March?

> Source K suggests that the march involved many people. It is clear that the marchers were Africans and that they were peaceful and orderly. It is also clear that the marchers were unarmed.

2/2. The response includes at least three good points. Because the maximum value for 13b is 2 marks for two good points, the response will be awarded 2 marks.

Exam practice

Now it's your turn to take a mock exam.

Read Sources M–P and answer questions 13–16 in the accompanying question paper. The sources and questions relate to Case study 2: Apartheid South Africa 1948–64 – protests and action: Sharpeville Massacre.

SOURCE M

Extract from Philip Frankel, *An Ordinary Atrocity: Sharpeville and its Massacre*, Yale University Press, New Haven, 2001, page 5. Frankel was the head of the Department of Political Science at the University of Witwatersrand, Johannesburg.

The Sharpeville massacre, historians concur, was not a 'benign' atrocity with few political consequences but a nefariously malignant event which instantly transformed the body politic of South Africa. The sheer horror of the killings that took place around Sharpeville Police Station on that fateful Monday made it virtually impossible for the international community to give any further moral leeway to the apartheid system, and although this did not mean an end to practical ties, after 21 March there were very few global actors who could be seen to be openly in league with South Africa … Within South Africa itself, the consequences of the Sharpeville massacre were manifold … After Sharpeville … it became impossible for the apartheid state to tolerate all but the most innocuous (and ineffectual) forms of black resistance. In a precursor of trends for the next thirty years Sharpeville initiated a violent state reaction against black political activity to which the African National Congress, the Pan Africanist Congress, the South African Communist Party and other opposition movements immediately fell victim.

SOURCE N

Photograph of Sharpeville burials, 1960, by Jürgen Schadeberg. Schadeberg is sometimes known as the 'father of South African photography'.

SOURCE O

Extract from UN Security Council Resolution 134 which passed on 1 April 1960. The vote was nine to none. France and Britain abstained (www.refworld.org/docid/3b00f1893c.html).

The Security Council,

Having considered the complaint of twenty-nine Member States ... concerning 'the situation arising out of the large-scale killings of unarmed and peaceful demonstrators against racial discrimination and segregation in the Union of South Africa' ...

2. *Deplores* that the recent disturbances in the Union of South Africa should have led to the loss of life of so many Africans and extends to the families of the victims its deepest sympathies;

3. *Deplores* the policies and actions of the Government of the Union of South Africa which have given rise to the present situation;

4. *Calls upon* the Government of the Union of South Africa to initiate measures aimed at bringing about racial harmony based on equality in order to ensure that the present situation does not continue or recur, and to abandon its policies of apartheid and racial discrimination ...

SOURCE P

Extract from Saul Dubow, *Apartheid 1948–1994*, Oxford University Press, Oxford, 2014, pages 81–2. Dubow is a professor of African History at the University of Cambridge. Dubow was born and raised in South Africa.

For a brief moment Sharpeville and Langa rocked the government. Huge quantities of foreign capital were repatriated overseas, the gold price and the stock market fell sharply, and the Finance Ministry was forced to take strong measures to protect against a deterioration in the government's reserves and its balance of payments ... The prospect of serious economic decline and the certainty of international isolation prompted alarm bordering on panic throughout South Africa. A state of emergency was declared in all the country's major urban areas as well as many rural districts, giving the police sweeping powers of arrest and detention. Parliament voted in favor of banning of the ANC and PAC, citing their allegedly revolutionary objectives. By the middle of May some 2,000 political leaders and activists, including Luthuli and Sobukwe, were taken into custody under the emergency regulations ...

13 a What, according to Source P, were the short-term effects of the Sharpeville Massacre? [3]
   b What does Source N suggest about the scale of the Sharpeville Massacre? [2]

14 With reference to its origin, purpose and content, analyse the value and limitations of Source O for a historian studying the UN response to Sharpeville. [4]

15 Compare and contrast how Sources M and P analyse the importance of Sharpeville. [6]

16 Using the sources and your own knowledge, examine why the international community was outraged by the Sharpeville Massacre. [9]

6 The role and significance of key actors/groups

Albert Luthuli (1898–1967)

Chief **Albert Luthuli** was one of the key anti-apartheid leaders in the 1950s and 1960s. Even though he spent much of these years under banning orders, he was still able to direct the actions of the African National Congress (ANC) and to help it grow into the most important South African movement fighting for equal rights. He was known widely for his moderate and tolerant outlook, as well as his fervent belief in non-violence.

■ Early life

Luthuli was born in neighbouring Rhodesia in 1898. His first work was as a teacher. In 1936, he became chief of the Zulu tribesmen near Groutville, Natal. Luthuli joined the ANC in 1944 and quickly became a member of the organization's Youth League. This group was active in pushing for more direct action against the segregation Africans faced in the years before apartheid became the law of the land. The group's actions ran counter to the older and more traditional ANC leadership. By 1951, Luthuli had become president of the Natal branch of the ANC. This would be his springboard to national prominence.

■ Luthuli as head of the ANC

In December 1952, Luthuli was elected as the president-general of the ANC. The South African authorities took notice and within months, Luthuli received the first of several banning orders:

- He was ordered to stay away from cities and public gatherings for one year.
- During the Defiance Campaign (see page 88), Luthuli was an active leader, speaking and organizing. The South African government told him he would have to resign either as chief or from his position in the ANC. Luthuli ignored the authorities and was soon dismissed as chief.
- Luthuli published his book *The Road to Freedom is Via the Cross* in November 1952. In it, he expounded on his deeply held Christian beliefs and why non-violence was the best path to resist apartheid. He made it quite clear that suffering was part of the struggle facing those opposed to the government's racial policies.

■ Banning

Luthuli was under a second banning order in July 1954:

- His movements were restricted to the small town of Stanger for two years.
- Nonetheless, in the wake of the 1955 Sophiatown removals (see page 78), Luthuli, from a distance, helped organize huge demonstrations protesting against the government actions.
- He was also not able to attend the Congress of the People when the Freedom Charter was adopted.
- The ban meant that Luthuli and other banned leaders had difficulties in staying in touch with the rank and file of the ANC and managing day-to-day planning since their movements were restricted.

Luthuli was one of the 156 people arrested and charged with treason and affiliation with the Communist Party in December 1956. Because the trial dragged on for so long, many ANC leaders were kept together. For the first time, they could meet and discuss consolidation of the anti-apartheid movement.

Even though Luthuli was eventually acquitted, he was banned for another five years, this time confined to his home. After the 1960 Sharpeville and Langa killings, Luthuli burned his pass book and called for a foreign boycott of South African goods. The ANC was outlawed shortly thereafter. Luthuli was awarded the 1960 Nobel Peace Prize and was allowed to leave the country briefly in December 1961 to accept the award in Oslo, Norway. His speech, *Africa and Freedom*, was well received but did little to alter the South African government's position. In 1962, Luthuli published his well-known *Let My People Go*, as well as a statement he wrote with Martin Luther King, Jr, entitled *Appeal for Action Against Apartheid*.

In 1964, he was issued with yet another five-year ban. He was hit and killed by a freight train near his home in 1967.

IDENTIFYING THE MAIN POINTS IN A SOURCE

- Question 13 of Paper 1 contains two parts, both of which test understanding of two different sources.
- Question 13a always refers to a narrative excerpt. Students are asked to identify main points from the source.
- This part of the question is worth 3 marks. That means three main points must be identified correctly. Do not go into too much detail. List at least three points. Three or four sentences are enough to fulfil the demands of this question.

Answer the question that follows each source below.

SOURCE A

Extract from Albert Luthuli's statement about the Rivonia Trial verdicts. Quoted in Gerald Pillay, *Voices of Liberation: Alfred Luthuli*, second edition, HSRC Press, Cape Town, 2014, page 138.

The African National Congress never abandoned its method of a militant, non-violent struggle, and of creating in the process a spirit of militancy in the people. However, in the face of the uncompromising white refusal to abandon a policy which denies the African and other oppressed South Africans their rightful heritage – freedom – no one can blame brave just men for seeking justice by the use of violent methods; nor could they be blamed if they tried to create an organised force in order ultimately to establish peace and racial harmony.

For this, they are sentenced to be shut away for long years in the brutal and degrading prisons of South Africa. With them will be interred [buried] this country's hopes for racial co-operation. They will leave a vacuum in leadership that may only be filled by bitter hate and racial strife.

SOURCE B

Extract from Albert Luthuli's speech in 1958 to a meeting organized by the South African Congress of Democrats in Johannesburg. Quoted in Gerald Pillay, *Voices of Liberation: Alfred Luthuli*, second edition, HSRC Press, Cape Town, 2014, pages 111–12.

Sometimes very nice and pretty phrases are used to justify this diversion from the democratic road. The one that comes to my mind is the suggestion that we Africans 'will develop along our own lines'. I do not know of any people who really have 'developed along their own lines'. My fellow white South Africans, enjoying what is called 'western civilisation', should be the first to agree that this civilisation is indebted to previous civilisations, from the East, from Greece, Rome and so on. For its heritage, western civilisation is really indebted to very many sources, both ancient and modern.

There is really no possibility of anyone developing 'along his own lines', as is often suggested. But in practice 'developing along your own lines' turns out not to be development along your own lines at all, but development along the lines designed by the government through the Native Affairs Department. Even in determining the laws that govern us and our development, there is no attempt to consult those who are affected. There is no contact between the governor and the governed at the present moment. 'Developing along our own lines' has come to mean 'developing along their lines – the government's lines'. The essence of development along your own lines is that you should have the right to develop, and the right to determine how to develop.

1 What, according to Source A, explains the reason that some ANC members had created a military force?
2 According to Source B, what are the weaknesses in the argument that Africans should develop 'along their own lines?'

Nelson Mandela (1918–2013)

■ Mandela's early life

Nelson Mandela was a member of the royal Thembu house, an important Xhosa-speaking group in South Africa. He was expected to become chief but instead went to the University of Fort Hare. He did not finish his degree there because he had been suspended for starting a student strike. He moved to Johannesburg and completed his degree by correspondence. In 1942, he earned his law degree from the University of Witwatersrand. Shortly thereafter, he joined the ANC.

■ Mandela and the ANCYL

Like many other young activists, Mandela was frustrated at the moderate positions taken by the ANC leadership. Consequently, he, along with Oliver Tambo, Walter Sisulu and Anton Lembede, formed the ANC Youth League (ANCYL) in September 1944. The group's programme of action included strikes, boycotts and other forms of non-compliance with racial laws. This was later adopted by the ANC in 1949.

■ Mandela as ANC leader

Mandela became a leading ANC activist and emerged as one of the organization's most influential leaders during the Defiance Campaign. He was the group's public spokesman and the 'volunteer-in-chief', whose responsibility was to enlist the volunteers needed to defy apartheid laws. Mandela was elected president of the ANCYL in 1952, as well head of the Transvaal ANC.

■ Arrests and bannings

Mandela faced continuous pressure from the authorities and was arrested and banned on several occasions. These included:

- 1952: arrested and charged with breaking the Suppression of Communism Act. While he received a suspended prison sentence, he was soon placed under a banning order.
- 1956: arrested and detained during the Treason Trial.
- 1960: arrested after the banning of the ANC. When he was released, he pushed for the creation of the ANC military wing, the *Umkhonto we Sizwe* (MK). He became a fugitive for the next seventeen months, hiding in South Africa and travelling abroad. The South African press dubbed him the **Black Pimpernel** after the fictional character the Scarlet Pimpernel who was so difficult to catch during the French Revolution.
- 1962: arrested when he returned to South Africa. Sentenced to five years in prison.
- 1963: while in prison, he was charged with sabotage in the Rivonia Trial. He was sentenced to life imprisonment. He remained in the penitentiary for non-white prisoners on Robben Island until 1990.

■ Impact of banning orders

Banning orders meant he was not free to travel or to meet with other ANC members. Even so, Mandela helped secretly plan all of the major ANC campaigns in the 1950s, including the Freedom Charter Campaign. At the People's Congress, he had to watch the proceedings surreptitiously from a nearby rooftop. At the All-in-African Conference held at Pietermaritzburg in March 1961, the 1400 delegates were thrilled when Mandela addressed them. Many had not heard him before because he had been banned from speaking in public for much of the previous decade. After the conference, he went underground.

■ Significance of Mandela

Among his many gifts, Mandela was an outstanding orator and organizer. With several other ANC luminaries such as Luthuli, Tambo and Sisulu, he helped the ANC grow from a small local organization that was out of touch with many South Africans into the largest and most active opponent of the apartheid regime. The ANC in the 1950s and early 1960s was at its peak of effectiveness. This was to change in the aftermath of Sharpeville with the banning of the organization and the arrest of much of its leadership.

DETERMINING THE VALUE AND LIMITATION OF A SOURCE'S CONTENT

● Question 14 will ask you to determine a source's value and limitations in regard to its origin, purpose and content.
Read the following source and answer the questions that follow.

SOURCE C

Extract from Nelson Mandela's statement to the press on 26 June 1961. It was published by the ANC in London (www. anc.org.za/content/struggle-my-life-nelson-mandelas-press-statement).

I am informed that a warrant for my arrest has been issued, and that the police are looking for me. The National Action Council has given full and serious consideration to this question … they have advised me not to surrender myself. I have accepted this advice, and will not give myself up to a government I do not recognise. Any serious politician will realise that under present-day conditions in this country, to seek for cheap martyrdom by handing myself to the police is naive and criminal. We have an important programme before us and it is important to carry it out very seriously and without delay.

I have chosen this latter course, which is more difficult and which entails more risk and hardship than sitting in gaol. I have had to separate myself from my dear wife and children, from my mother and sisters, to live as an outlaw in my own land. I have had to close my business, to abandon my profession, and live in poverty and misery, as many of my people are doing. I will continue to act as the spokesman of the National Action Council during the phase that is unfolding and in the tough struggles that lie ahead. I shall fight the government side by side with you, inch by inch, and mile by mile, until victory is won. What are you going to do? Will you come along with us, or are you going to co-operate with the government in its efforts to suppress the claims and aspirations of your own people? Or are you going to remain silent and neutral in a matter of life and death to my people, to our people? For my own part I have made my choice. I will not leave South Africa, nor will I surrender. Only through hardship, sacrifice and militant action can freedom be won. The struggle is my life. I will continue fighting for freedom until the end of my days.

3   Why wouldn't Mandela turn himself in to the authorities?
4   How had Mandela suffered?
5   What is the value of the content of this source for a historian studying Nelson Mandela?

EXAMINING A VISUAL SOURCE

● Question 13b will ask students to determine the significance of a visual source.

Look at the following photo closely and answer the question that follows.

6   What does Source D suggest about Nelson Mandela at the Treason Trial?

SOURCE D

Mandela at the Treason Trial in 1958. Photograph by Jürgen Schadeberg.

Other significant individuals

The ANC and PAC possessed many outstanding leaders and activists. Among them were the following.

■ Oliver Tambo (1917–93)

Oliver Tambo was one of the founding members of the ANCYL. Milestones in his life were:

- 1951: Tambo and Mandela set up the first African law firm in South Africa.
- 1953: Tambo was appointed national secretary of the ANC in the place of Walter Sisulu, who had been banned.
- 1954: after he was elected secretary general of the ANC, he received a banning order.
- 1960: when the ANC was banned after Sharpeville, Tambo fled South Africa and created the ANC Mission in Exile. He pushed for economic sanctions against South Africa and helped set up training camps for ANC military groups.
- 1990: Tambo returned to South Africa after the unbanning of the ANC.

■ Walter Sisulu (1912–2003)

Sisulu was also a founding member of the ANCYL. He held several important ANC posts and was arrested seven times. He was a defendant at the Treason Trial. After the authorities banned the ANC, Sisulu was arrested. While out on bail, he went into hiding. He was one of those caught at the Rivonia farmhouse. At the ensuing Rivonia Trial, he was sentenced to life in prison.

Among his major accomplishments were his tireless efforts to transform the ANC into a mass-based militant organization. Sisulu was also key in forging very close ties with the South African Communist Party and for helping set up the armed resistance, *Umkhonto we Sizwe* (MK).

■ Robert Sobukwe (1924–78)

Sobukwe joined the ANC in 1950 and soon began to disagree with the organization's multiracial character. Sobukwe was firmly convinced that an Africanist approach was better. This meant that the ANC should act in the interests of black South Africans and that they were part of a greater African struggle to free themselves from white domination. In 1959, Sobukwe created the Pan Africanist Congress (PAC).

Sobukwe was a natural leader and a persuasive speaker. He wanted to rival the ANC and so pushed for the anti-pass demonstrations a week before the ANC's in 1960. This led to the Sharpeville Massacre. The South African authorities found him to be a great threat since he wanted nothing less than the total destruction of the apartheid state and had set up the armed group *Poqo*. Consequently, the authorities banned him in 1960 and then sentenced him to prison for three years for inciting Africans to demand the repeal of pass laws.

At the end of September 1963, the South African Parliament enacted the General Law Amendment Act and included the 'Sobukwe Clause'. This permitted the minister of justice to prolong detention of any political prisoner indefinitely. The clause was never used to detain anyone else but Sobukwe. He was kept in solitary confinement until his release in 1969.

EXAMINING THE ORIGIN OF A SOURCE

- Question 14 of Paper 1 requires students to evaluate the value and limitations of a source based on its origin, purpose and content.
- The origin of a source comes from several components: author, title, date of origin, type of source, and, if applicable, title, publisher and type of publication.
- Information about origin can be found in the description of a source that precedes the source's text.
- The following questions are designed to make connections between the components of a source's origin and how they affect value or limitation.

Refer to Source D to answer the questions below. Use the topic: for a historian studying the role and significance of key groups. Use the table below to help you formulate your answer.

SOURCE D

Extract from Robert Sobukwe's opening address to the Pan Africanist Congress (PAC) on 4 April 1959. Sobukwe made it clear how the PAC's ideas differed from the multiracial outlook of the ANC (www.sahistory.org.za/archive/document-58-robert-mangaliso-sobukwe-opening-address-africanist-inaugural-convention-4-april).

Against multi-racialism we have this objection, that the history of South Africa has fostered group prejudices and antagonisms, and if we have to maintain the same group exclusiveness, parading under the term of multi-racialism, we shall be transporting to the new Africa these very antagonisms and conflicts. Further, multi-racialism is in fact a pandering to European bigotry and arrogance. It is a method of safeguarding white interests irrespective of population figures. In that sense it is a complete negation of democracy. To us the term 'multi-racialism' implies that there are such basic insuperable differences between the various national groups here that the best course is to keep them permanently distinctive in a kind of democratic apartheid. That to us is racialism multiplied, which probably is what the term truly connotes.

We aim, politically, at a government of the Africans by the Africans for Africans, with everybody who owes his only loyalty to Africa and who is prepared to accept the democratic rule of an African majority being regarded as an African. We guarantee no minority rights, because we think in terms of individuals, not groups.

7   Who is the author of Source D?
8   In what ways does Sobukwe's role as the founder of the Pan Africanist Congress provide value to this source for a historian studying the role and significance of key groups?
9   In what ways is Sobukwe's position in the Pan Africanist Congress a limitation to a historian studying the role and significance of key groups?

	Key information	Value	Limitations
Author			
Title			
Date of origin			
Type of source			
Publisher information			

The African National Congress (ANC)

■ The early years of the ANC

The most prominent South African organization fighting for black African rights was the African National Congress (ANC). At a meeting in Bloemfontein in 1912, the South African Native National Congress was formed with Solomon Plaatje as its head. In 1923, the group became the ANC. In the inter-war period, the ANC's middle-class leadership was seen as being out of touch with the realities of most Africans. The group had difficulty in bridging the wide tribal and language differences to create a unified movement. Even though the ANC produced many well-researched studies on the impact of segregation in South Africa, most Africans were illiterate.

■ The ANC Youth League (ANCYL)

In the 1940s, a group within the ANC formed the Youth League. The ANCYL tried to broaden the base with mass support, as well as to instigate new approaches to combating the segregation in South African society. Shortly after the National Party won the 1948 elections, promising to introduce even more comprehensive laws separating the races, the ANCYL drew up its Programme of Action in 1949. The programme:

- rejected white domination
- supported African nationalism in South Africa and in the rest of the colonized continent
- called for mass protests
- fostered African pride to counter the notion of white supremacy.

■ Tensions in the ANC

The ANC adopted this as its own platform. Within the ANC there were tensions that threatened the unity of the organization. Some members were called the Africanists. They believed that the ANC should not cooperate with other racial groups but should focus solely on the struggle for civil rights from an African perspective. The Africanists broke from the ANC and formed their own organization, the Pan Africanist Congress (PAC). Other ANC members thought that the more support they had from other groups would be the best approach to countering the Afrikaner apartheid legislations. Hence, the ANC signed a cooperation pact with the Natal Indian Congress and the Transvaal Indian Congress, known as the 'Three Doctors' Pact', in 1947.

The ANC was most active in the 1950s, fighting apartheid at every step. Among its many campaigns were the following:

- The 1952 Defiance Campaign. Along with the South African Indian Congress, the ANC protested against the introduction of new apartheid laws. Thousands went to jail for breaking the law. The ANC's Women's League was deeply involved in this campaign.
- Boycott of Bantu schools in 1955. Because there was no viable alternative, the campaign failed.
- The 1955 Congress of People at Kliptown. The Freedom Charter was adopted here. By the year's end, 42 ANC leaders had been banned.
- The anti-pass for women campaign. In 1955, the government announced that at the start of 1956, women, too, would have to carry passes. On 9 August, 20,000 women marched in Pretoria against the new measure.
- The Alexandra Bus Boycott of 1957.

The South African government tried to disrupt the actions of the ANC by arrests, banning orders, beatings and long, drawn-out court cases such as the Treason Trial and the Rivonia Trial. The government also outlawed the group in 1960, which drove many activists underground. In reaction, and desperation, the ANC formed its military wing, and began a series of attacks on government installations. With the lifetime sentences of some of its top leaders at the end of the Rivonia Trial, though, the organization was crippled.

SUMMARIZING A SOURCE

- Question 16 of Paper 1 requires students to integrate knowledge from four sources and their own knowledge in response to a question about a topic from the one of the case studies in Rights and protest.
- A successful response requires students to integrate summaries of sources.
- A good summary is based upon the main ideas of a source.
- The main idea of a source can be identified using relevant content or identifying how relevant content is connected by a bigger idea or concept.

Read Source E below and then answer the questions that follow. Limit each answer to one sentence in length.

SOURCE E

Extract from Nelson Mandela's speech 'On Tribalism', May 1959. Quoted in Nelson Mandela, *No Easy Walk to Freedom*, Heinemann International, Oxford, 1989, pages 77–8.

The leading organization of the African people is the African National Congress. Congress has repeatedly denounced apartheid. It has repeatedly endorsed the Freedom Charter, which claims South Africa 'for all its people'. It is true that occasionally individual Africans become so depressed and desperate at Nationalist misrule that they have tended to clutch at any straw to say: give us any little corner where we may be free to run our own affairs. But Congress has always firmly rejected such momentary tendencies and refused to barter our birthright, which is South Africa, for such illusory 'Bantustans' …

There is no need for Dr. Eiselen … or others to argue about 'what Africans think' about the future of this country. Let the people speak for themselves! Let us have a free vote and a free election of delegates to a national convention, irrespective of colour or nationality. Let the Nationalists submit their plan, and the Congress its Charter. If Verwoerd and Eiselen think the Africans support their schemes they need not fear such a procedure. If they are not prepared to submit to public opinion, then let them stop parading and pretending to the outside world that they are democrats, and talking revolting nonsense about 'Bantu self-government'.

10 What role has the ANC played in fighting apartheid?

11 Why have some Africans supported the Nationalist government?

12 What does Mandela think the Nationalists should do?

MIND MAP

- The ANC may be the topic of a Paper 1 exam.
- Even if it is not a specific topic, the many connections that can be made to the trial make it potentially useful as own knowledge for the last question of a Paper 1 exam requiring students to use all four sources and their own knowledge.

Use the information from the opposite page to add details to the mind map below.

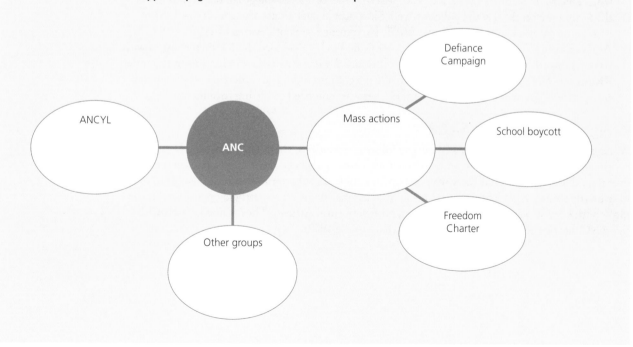

The South African Communist Party (SACP)

Revised ☐

■ The foundation of the Communist Party of South Africa

The Communist Party of South Africa (CPSA) was created in 1921. It was primarily concerned with trade union disputes and organized many strikes in its early years. Like communist parties around the world, the CPSA took its orders directly from the Soviet Union. The party was the only South African one which actively sought African members. It believed that divisions in society were along class and not racial lines.

■ CPSA–ANC relations

Relations between the CPSA and the ANC were not always smooth. Many ANC members were devout Christians and could not imagine working together with the communists. For their part, many communists thought the ANC was a bourgeois organization that would not dramatically change South Africa. This situation changed in the late 1940s as a new group of ANC leaders began to take charge of their organization. From this point on, the two organizations often worked closely together to plan mass campaigns.

■ Important events in the history of the SACP

Among the milestones in the party's history are the following:

- In 1950, the South African Parliament discussed a legislative measure called the Unlawful Organizations bill that would have outlawed the CPSA. In response, the Free Speech Convention organized by the CPSA, ANC, Indian Congress and African People's Organisation was held in March 1950. Five hundred delegates met to voice their protest and 10,000 attended a rally afterwards.
- The May Day Massacre in 1950. Eighteen CPSA members were gunned down by the police while striking. The ANC declared a national day of mourning for the victims.
- Just before Parliament passed the new version of the Unlawful Organizations bill, now known as the Suppression of Communism Act, the CPSA dissolved itself. Some members created a new political party called the Congress of Democrats while other communists went underground and renamed their party the South African Communist Party (SACP) in 1953.
- In 1952, the one communist member in Parliament, Sam Khan, was expelled from the legislature.
- In 1955, the communist Joe Slovo was a key contributor to writing the Freedom Charter.
- Many communists were charged in the Treason Trial in 1956.
- When the police raided the farmhouse in Rivonia, several communists were among those arrested. The SACP worked together with the ANC to create the semi-independent military wing, *Umkhonto we Sizwe* (MK). Joe Slovo was the chief of staff of the group but he was not at the farmhouse on the day the police arrived. Slovo would later escape the country in 1963 to help set up external groups to help the SACP. He returned to South Africa in 1990.
- At the Rivonia Trial in 1963–4, the Afrikaner Bram Fischer defended the ten men charged with trying to overthrow the government. The authorities did not know that Fischer was in the inner Rivonia circle. Fischer was later arrested in 1964, went into hiding, and then arrested again for conspiracy to overthrow the government. Fischer was sentenced to life imprisonment.

■ Significance of the SACP

While the CPSA and then the SACP were small-scale operations, the South African government continually portrayed them as extremely dangerous, particularly because of their supposed influence over the ANC. The National Party whipped up anti-communist hysteria whenever possible in order to scare the whites into adopting even harsher restrictions on any anti-apartheid opposition. In the ranks of the SACP were many gifted activists, both white and African. They worked closely with the ANC during the peak of anti-apartheid activity in the 1950s.

EXAMINING THE PURPOSE OF A SOURCE

- Question 14 requires students to evaluate the value and limitations of a source based on its origin, purpose and content.
- The purpose of a source refers to why the author created the source.
- Knowing why a source was created can provide some insight into what kind of information was included and what kind of information may have been omitted.
- It also may give an indication to the perspective of the author.

Read Source F and then answer the questions that follow.

SOURCE F

Extract from Nelson Mandela's speech when he awarded the ANC's highest honour to Joe Slovo in December 1994 (www.sacp.org.za/main.php?ID=2671).

Comrade Joe Slovo, your militant and unswerving commitment to the ANC embodies many values which we wish to honour today. There are some people who, by pursuing their own convictions and without being self-conscious about it, touch the lives of millions of others. Such has been your life.

I am not sure, comrade Joe, if you have ever particularly thought of yourself as a white South African. Nevertheless, the fact remains that your decades of activism have served as an outstanding example for hundreds of thousands of activists coming into our ranks, and indeed for millions of other South Africans …

Comrade Joe, you also symbolise and personify the alliance of the ANC and the SACP. It is an alliance whose durability continues to bewilder our opponents. They fail to understand its deep historical roots and its ongoing practical relevance …

Your contributions to our struggle are many. But it is, I think, especially as a strategic thinker that you are held most dear by so many in our ranks. You have played a role, often a central role, in most of the outstanding strategic documents of our struggle. In the decades of exile, I know that yours was a crucial role in the regrouping and consolidation of Umkhonto we Sizwe.

13 Why did Nelson Mandela make this speech?
14 What might some limitations be in this source for a historian studying the ANC–SACP alliance?

INTEGRATING KNOWLEDGE AND SOURCES

- Question 16 of Paper 1 requires students to integrate knowledge from four sources and their own knowledge in response to a question about a topic from the one of the case studies in Rights and protest.

Using Sources A–F found in Chapter 6, identify relevant content to help answer the question.

Examine the role played by key individuals and groups in confronting the apartheid regime.

Use the table below to record a brief summary of the relevant content from each source.

Source	Brief summary
Source A	
Source B	
Source C	
Source D	
Source E	
Source F	

Exam focus

Exam practice

Now it's your turn to take a mock exam.

Read Sources M–P and answer questions 13–16 in the accompanying question paper. The sources and questions relate to Case study 2: Apartheid South Africa 1948–64 – the role and significance of key actors/groups: Nelson Mandela.

SOURCE M

Extract from Elleke Boehmer, *Nelson Mandela: A Very Short Introduction*, Oxford University Press, Oxford, 2008, pages 123–4. Boehmer is a professor of World Literature at Oxford University. She is recognized for her research on colonial and postcolonial literature.

At his trials in both 1962 and 1964 Mandela chose, after consultation, to represent himself in the dock, thinking that the direct form of address this afforded him would create an ideal opportunity for broadcasting the political vision of the already-banned ANC. In this he was massively successful. His two strategically planned and rhetorically patterned speeches propelled the African nationalists' anti-apartheid fight in South Africa on to the world stage, and, moreover, shone the historical limelight centrally on Mandela … Not for nothing was he called the Black Pimpernel … He is said not to have resented the appellation. It appealed to his sense of himself as able to establish rapport with a variety of different audiences – 'with Muslims in the Cape … sugar-workers in Natal … factory workers in Port Elizabeth', he writes in his autobiography. It appealed also to his desire for mastery of any situation in which he might find himself … For an exiled movement in need of messianic leadership, Mandela fitted the bill perfectly and, indeed, was happy to style his image so as to advance the nationalist cause.

SOURCE N

Photo from *Drum* magazine, February 1957. The photo was taken near the Johannesburg courthouse for the Treason Trial. An estimated 5000 demonstrators protested against the trial of the 156 men and women charged with treason.

SOURCE O

Extract from Saul Dubow, *Apartheid 1948–1994*, Oxford University Press, Oxford, 2014, pages 96–7. Dubow is a professor of African History at the University of Cambridge. Dubow was born and raised in South Africa.

Mandela decided to turn the courtroom into a trial of the apartheid state itself, arguing that his actions were guided by his conscience. He made use of a legal convention that allowed him to address the court from the dock, rather than entering the witness stand. This allowed him to speak to the world, not just the courtroom, and to do so from a position of strength and without cross-examination. The presence of many foreign journalists and the active interest of the United Nations gave Mandela a unique opportunity to immortalize, even sacralize [make sacred], a struggle whose future was, to say the least, uncertain.

In the course of a brilliantly crafted speech … Mandela reviewed the history of the ANC and his own personal development. He anticipated possible martyrdom with extraordinary dignity and grace. Mandela began by disavowing the state's charge that the struggle was being manipulated by foreigners or Communists: 'I have done whatever I did, both as an individual and as a leader of my people, because of my own proudly felt African background, and not because of what any outsider may have said.'

SOURCE P

Extract from Nelson Mandela, *The Struggle is My Life*, Pathfinder Press, Atlanta, 1990, page 88. The following is from Mandela's testimony in 1960 at the Treason Trial, which ran from 1956 to 1960. Mandela was acquitted.

BENCH [the judge]: Mandela, assuming … do you visualise any future action on behalf of the Government, by the Government? Because I think the evidence suggests that you could not expect the Government to soften in its views. Have you any future plans in that event?

MANDELA: No, my lord. I don't think that the Congress has ever believed that its policy of pressure would ultimately fail. The Congress, of course, does not expect that one single push to coerce the Government to change its policy will succeed; the Congress expects that over a period, as a result of a repetition of these pressures, together with world opinion, that the Government notwithstanding its attitude of ruling Africans with an iron hand, that … the methods which we are using will bring about a realisation of our aspirations.

PROSECUTION: Mr. Mandela, whether or not there would be success ultimately, one thing is clear, is it not, and that is that the African National Congress held the view, and propagated the view, that in resisting pressure by the Congress Movement the ruling class, the Government, would not hesitate to retaliate – would not hesitate to use violence and armed force against the Congress Movement?

MANDELA: Yes, the Congress was of that view, my lords. We did expect force to be used, as far as the Government is concerned, but as far as we are concerned we took the precautions to ensure that that violence will not come from our side.

13 a What, according to Source M, did Mandela hope to accomplish in his testimony? [3]
b What does Source N suggest about the public reaction to the Treason Trial? [2]

14 With reference to its origin, purpose and content, analyse the value and limitations of Source P for a historian studying the Treason Trial. [4]

15 Compare and contrast how Sources M and O explain Mandela's aims during his trials. [6]

16 Using the sources and your own knowledge, discuss Mandela's role in the ANC. [9]

Glossary

14th Amendment This guaranteed 'equal protection of the law' to all citizens.

15th Amendment This granted the suffrage to black men. (Women, black and white, were granted the right to vote in 1920.)

AFL-CIO The American Federation of Labor and Congress of Industrial Organizations were merged to create the largest federation of unions in the USA.

African Nationalism The movement within Africa for independence from colonial powers such as Britain and for civil and political rights in South Africa.

Africans The original black population of Africa.

Afrikaners Descendants of immigrants to South Africa, mainly from the Netherlands and Germany.

Amendments Under the Constitution, Congress could make changes, in the form of new clauses, to the Constitution. Each Amendment required a two-thirds majority in Congress and approval by 75% of the states.

Apartheid Strict separation of different racial groups. It is an Afrikaans word, meaning 'separate' or 'apartness'.

Attorney general Head of the Justice Department in the federal government.

Baasskap Afrikaner term used to describe their power over so-called 'inferior' races, loosely meaning: 'do as I say because I'm the boss'.

Bail A payment demanded by a court of law in order to release a person awaiting trial. If not paid, the person must stay in custody.

Banning orders Orders by which individuals or groups were banned from certain areas or from contacting others, or forced to live in specific areas.

Bantu An African people who speak a common group of languages. In the apartheid era, the white minority used 'Bantu' or 'native' to refer to Africans in South Africa, often in a derogatory way.

Bantustans Areas in South Africa set aside for Africans. Sometimes referred to as 'tribal homelands' or 'homelands'.

Black Monday What many southerners called 17 May 1954, the day the Supreme Court released the *Brown v. Board of Education* decision.

Black nationalists Those who believed that black people should seek separation from, not integration with, whites. Many of them criticized the policy of non-violence.

Black Pimpernel Referring to the Scarlet Pimpernel, the elusive hero of Baroness Orczy's novels set during the French Revolution.

'Black spots' Areas outside the land officially designated for settlement by black Africans where they nevertheless managed to acquire land.

Border states Originally, the slave states that did not leave the Union in 1861. They included Delaware, Kentucky, Maryland and Missouri.

Boycott A refusal to have anything to do with a person or an organization.

Brown v. Board of Education of Topeka Supreme Court case that determined that states could not establish separate schools according to race.

Cape The southernmost province of South Africa, originally Cape Colony, part of the British Empire.

Capital Citizens' Council White group set up to resist desegregation of schools in Little Rock, Arkansas.

Civil Rights Movement A range of social and political movements in the USA whose goal was to end racial segregation and discrimination against black Americans and ensure legal, social and political equality for them.

Commonwealth Association of members and former members of the British Empire.

Communist A person who believes that the planning and control of the economy should be by the state and people should be rewarded according to the value of their contribution.

Communist Party of South Africa (CPSA) Communist Party believing in ideas such as state ownership of industry and equality for everyone.

Confederacy The eleven southern slave-holding states which declared independence from the USA in 1861. A bitter civil war from 1861 to 1865 was fought to reunite the nation.

Congress The national, or federal, law-making body.

Congress of Racial Equality (CORE) An interracial civil rights group founded by James Farmer and other students in Chicago in 1942.

Deep South Used to denote the states which had been most dependent on plantation agriculture, sometimes referred to as the Cotton Belt, and which had formed the core of the Confederacy. It is usually thought to include states such as Alabama, Louisiana, Mississippi and South Carolina.

De facto In reality.

De jure Based on laws of the state.

Delegations Groups meeting those in authority to make specific requests.

Department of Native Affairs The South African government department that regulated the lives of black citizens.

Desegregation The (process of) ending of segregation or the implementation of integration.

Direct action Action to protest about something, for example a march or demonstration.

Disenfranchised Deprived of the right to vote.

Dominion Largely self-governing country within the British Empire, recognizing the monarch as head of state.

Dutch Reformed Church Afrikaner Church which supported apartheid.

Federal Bureau of Investigation (FBI) The main investigative branch of the federal Department of Justice.

Federal system of government A system in which power is shared between central and state governments.

Federalized To come under the control of the US government.

Filibuster Delaying tactic in legislative process to stop a bill from being passed.

Forced removals Where black, coloured or Indian people were removed from areas designated 'whites only' and forced to live in locations or townships, usually on the edge of urban areas.

Freedom Riders Volunteers who challenged segregation in interstate bus terminals in the South in 1961.

Ghetto An area inhabited overwhelmingly by (usually poor) members of one race or ethnic group.

Grand apartheid Policies to keep different races as separated as possible.

Great Society President Johnson's plan to decrease poverty and inequality in the USA.

Guerrilla warfare Fighting using techniques such as ambush and bombings, avoiding direct large-scale conflict.

Historically Black Colleges and Universities (HBCU) Educational institutions mostly set up after the Civil War to educate freed slaves. More than 100 are still open today.

Homelands Areas laid aside for Africans to live in according to their tribal groups.

'Jim Crow' laws Named after a comic, stereotypical character, these laws were passed by southern states in order to 'legalize' segregation.

Ku Klux Klan (KKK) A secret terrorist society formed by ex-Confederate soldiers in 1865 in order to maintain white supremacy.

Legislature The elected, law-making body in each state (the state equivalent of Congress).

Litigation Taking a case to a court of law.

Little Rock Nine Nine high school students who were the first black students to attend Central High School in Little Rock, Arkansas in 1957.

Lynching Unlawful killing, mostly by hanging, usually of black people.

Mission schools Schools run by various Churches to educate African children.

Montgomery Bus Boycott Black bus riders in Montgomery, Alabama refused to ride city buses for 381 days in 1956–7 until segregated seating ended.

Montgomery Improvement Association (MIA) The organization that co-ordinated the Montgomery Bus Boycott.

Nation of Islam (NOI) A religious movement founded in 1930. Its leader was Elijah Muhammad and its main stated goal was to improve the lives of African Americans in the USA.

National Association for the Advancement of Colored People (NAACP) The oldest and largest civil rights organization. It is still active today.

National Party South African political party which won the 1948 elections. Its platform was based on segregationist policies. It stayed in power until 1994.

Pan Africanist Congress (PAC) Black African organization that set up an Africanist agenda, in which the government of South Africa should comprise only black Africans.

Pass books Internal passports to restrict the movement of people.

Petitioned Presented an appeal bearing the signatures of as many supporters as possible.

Petty apartheid Day-to-day restrictions keeping the races separated.

Plessy v. Ferguson 1896 Supreme Court decision that upheld racial segregation as long as public facilities were 'equal'.

Poll tax A tax levied on would-be voters, which made it harder for black people (who were usually poorer) to vote.

Reconstruction The process of rebuilding and reforming the Confederate states and restoring them to the Union.

Second World War Fought from 1939 and 1945 between the Allies, primarily the USA, the UK, France and the USSR (Union of Soviet Socialist Republics, or the Soviet Union), and Nazi Germany, Japan and their allies.

Segregation The separation of people by race in schools and public spaces and on transport.

Shanty towns Areas made up of temporary, often inadequate accommodation and lacking proper facilities such as sanitation or supplies of fresh water.

Southern Christian Leadership Conference (SCLC) A non-violent civil rights organization founded by Martin Luther King, Jr.

Southern Manifesto A statement of defiance against the 1954 *Brown* ruling which was signed by most southerners in Congress.

Soviet Union The leading Communist country from 1922 to 1991.

Student Nonviolent Coordinating Committee (SNCC) The student-run organization formed after the 1960 sit-ins.

Supreme Court The highest court in the USA. Its primary role was to interpret the Constitution.

Townships Areas where black people lived separately from other races.

Transvaal Indian Congress (TIC) Branch of the South African Indian Congress (SAIC) based in Transvaal.

Umkhonto we Sizwe Spear of the Nation (MK) – the armed wing of the ANC.

United Nations (UN) An organization formed in 1945, the main aim of which was to solve international disputes.

White supremacy The belief that white people are superior to other races.

Key figures

Baker, Ella (1903–86) Important civil rights activist. While serving as the executive secretary of the Southern Christian Leadership Conference (SCLC), she pushed for the creation of a student-centred organization. The Student Nonviolent Coordinating Committee (SNCC) was subsequently formed.

Johnson, Lyndon B. (1908–73) US president who signed into law two of the most important civil rights bills: the 1964 Civil Rights Act and the 1965 Voting Rights Act.

King, Martin Luther, Jr (1929–68) Civil rights leader and head of the Southern Christian Leadership Conference (SCLC). King was the most well-known black leader in the 1950s and 1960s. He participated in some of the key events of the anti-segregation struggle, including the Montgomery Bus Boycott, the Selma to Montgomery March and the March on Washington.

Luthuli, Albert (1898–1967) Luthuli was the president-general of the African National Congress (ANC) from 1952 to 1967. He was the most widely known South African leader during this period. Luthuli worked tirelessly to end apartheid in South Africa.

Malan, D.F. (1874–1959) Malan was the first National Party prime minister. It was under his rule, 1946–54, that many of the apartheid laws were passed.

Malcolm X (1925–65) Black nationalist and Nation of Islam (NOI) leader. Malcolm X promoted black pride and harshly criticized racism in the USA.

Mandela, Nelson (1918–2013) African National Congress (ANC) leader and anti-apartheid revolutionary. Mandela was active in most of the major ANC campaigns in the 1950s. His final term in prison lasted for 27 years.

Marshall, Thurgood (1908–93) Lawyer for the National Association for the Advancement of Colored People (NAACP). Marshall argued some of the most significant cases that helped end Jim Crow segregation.

Parks, Rosa (1913–2005) National Association for the Advancement of Colored People (NAACP) activist who refused to surrender her seat to a white passenger in Montgomery, Alabama. Her subsequent arrest set off the Montgomery Bus Boycott, an event that some historians mark as the beginning of the Civil Rights Movement.

Verwoerd, Hendrik (1901–66) South African politician who was prime minister from 1958 to 1966. He was a rigid supporter of apartheid.

Warren, Earl (1891–1974) Chief justice of the US Supreme Court from 1953 to 1969. Warren presided over many important civil rights cases during this period.

Timeline

The Civil Rights Movement in the United States 1954–65

1863	Emancipation Proclamation
1865	Dec: 13th Amendment abolished slavery
1866	Ku Klux Klan founded
1868	July: 14th Amendment guaranteed 'equal protection of the law' to all citizens
1870	March: 15th Amendment granted black male suffrage
1881	First Jim Crow laws passed
1890	Mississippi became first state to disenfranchise blacks
1896	May: *Plessy v. Ferguson* ruled that 'separate but equal' treatment of the races was not unconstitutional
1909	NAACP formed
1941	June: President Roosevelt banned discrimination in war industries after Randolph threatened March on Washington
1943	Race riot in Detroit
1948	President Truman ordered desegregation in armed forces
1954	May: *Brown v. Board of Education* ruled that segregation in education was unconstitutional
	July: First White Citizens' Council formed
1955	May: *'Brown II'* ruling called for desegregation in education 'with all deliberate speed'
	Aug: Emmett Till murdered
	Dec: Start of Montgomery Bus Boycott
1956	March: Southern Manifesto
	Dec: Successful end to Montgomery Bus Boycott
1957	Jan: Southern Christian Leadership Conference (SCLC) formed
	Sept: Civil Rights Act passed
	Dec: President Eisenhower sent federal troops into Little Rock, Arkansas

1959	TV programme *The Hate that Hate Produced* about Malcolm X and Nation of Islam (NOI)
1960	Feb: Sit-ins began
	April: Student Nonviolent Coordinating Committee (SNCC) formed
	May: Civil Rights Act
1961	May: Freedom Rides began
	Nov: Albany Movement began Start of SNCC campaign in Mississippi
1962	Sept: 'Battle of Ole Miss'
1963	SCLC campaign in Birmingham, Alabama
	June: Kennedy's speech called civil rights a 'moral issue' and sent a civil rights bill to Congress
	Aug: March on Washington
	Nov: Assassination of President Kennedy
1964	Mississippi Freedom Democratic Party (MFDP) organized
	July: Civil Rights Act passed
	Nov: Johnson won presidential election
1965	Feb: Assassination of Malcolm X
	March: Selma–Montgomery march led to 'Bloody Sunday'
	Aug: Voting Rights Act passed. Race riots erupted in Watts, Los Angeles

Apartheid South Africa 1948–64

1910	May: Creation of the Union of South Africa
1912	Jan: Formation of the South African Native National Congress (SANNC), renamed the African National Congress (ANC) in 1923
1913	June: Natives Land Act
1919	Industrial and Commercial Union (ICU) formed
1921	South African Indian Congress (SAIC) formed
1923	June: Urban Areas Act
1927	Sept: Native Administration Act
1935	March: All-African Convention formed
1936	Aug: Native Trust and Land Act
1938	Dec: Celebration of centenary of the Great Trek
1944	April: Youth League of the ANC formed
1947	March: 'Three Doctors' Pact' between ANC and SAIC
1948	May: National Party electoral victory
1950	July: Population Registration Act
	July: Group Areas Act
1951	July: Bantu Authorities Act
1952	Native Laws Amendment Act
	April–Dec: Defiance Campaign
1953	Reservation of Separate Amenities Act
1954	Jan: Bantu Education Act
	April: Federation of African Women formed
1955	Feb: Destruction of Sophiatown began
	June: Freedom Charter adopted
1956	March: Separate Representation of Voters Act passed
	Dec: Mass arrests in preparation for the Treason Trial

1957	Jan–June: Alexandra Bus Boycott
1959	April: Pan African Congress (PAC) formed
	Aug: Treason Trial finally began Extension of Universities Act Promotion of Self-Government Act
1960	March: Sharpeville Massacre
	April–Aug: State of emergency declared
	April: ANC and PAC made illegal
	April: Assassination attempt on Prime Minister Hendrik Verwoerd
1961	Jan: East Pondoland rebellion suppressed
	March: Treason Trial ended
	March: South Africa became a republic
	June: Spear of the Nation (MK) formed
	June: South Africa left the Commonwealth
	July: John Vorster appointed minister of justice
	Dec: Chief Luthuli, president of the ANC, won the Nobel Peace Prize
1962	Aug: Nelson Mandela arrested
	June: Sabotage Act
	Nov: *Poqo* attack on town of Paarl
	Dec: First ANC bombings on government buildings
1963	May: General Laws Amendment Act – 90-day rule
	May: Transkei became the first self-governing Bantustan
	July: Government raid on Liliesleaf Farm
	Oct: Rivonia Trial began
1964	Bantu Laws Amendment Act
	June: Rivonia Trial ended – defendants found guilty and sentenced to life imprisonment

Answers

■ Case study 1: The Civil Rights Movement in the United States 1954–65

■ 1 Nature and characteristics of discrimination

■ Page 9, Identifying relevant content

1 The main goals of the Jim Crow laws were to create a legal system to separate the races and protect white people. The harsh laws and fear were needed to keep the black people in 'their place'. The laws would also preserve the 'southern way of life and uphold God's law'.

■ Page 11, Content comprehension

2 Race mixing, according to Eldon Edwards, would destroy both the white and black races. It would also result in the end of the USA. He also claimed that if a white person had even the smallest amount of non-white blood, his white blood would be destroyed forever.

■ Page 13, Identifying relevant content from an illustration

3 Source C points out that the person responsible for administering literacy tests is illiterate himself since he asks what the word 'literacy' means. Source C also suggests that an officer of the law oversees the process as the man on the left is wearing a badge. Finally, the source shows that both men are white and they would be the ones a black person hoping to register would have to face.

■ Page 15, Examining the content of a source

4 The source is from a 1985 interview with Melba Beals, one of the Little Rock Nine students. It was part of the TV documentary *Eyes on the Prize* and was first broadcast in 1987.

5 Because this interview is from one of the original participants in the Little Rock desegregation effort, it is very valuable to historians. The interview records Beals' insights about her experiences.

6 The interview was conducted 28 years after the events Beals describes. In the intervening years, her memory of events could have changed. The excerpt does not include the question so we may not have a full sense of the extent to which Beals answered the question.

■ Page 17, Examining the content of a source

7 This source is valuable for historians because it clearly states the reaction of the NAACP to the *Brown* decision. The Atlanta Declaration lays out what the next steps needed are. The content's limitations include the one-sided and very optimistic view of the impact the *Brown* verdict would have.

■ Page 19, Examining the purpose of a source

8 The purpose of the source has value for historians because the Southern Manifesto was issued publicly by southern congressmen in order to show their full opposition to the Supreme Court decision. It put others in Congress on notice that virtually the whole southern delegation was against desegregation of schools. The limitation of the purpose might be that because it was a public statement in Congress, the congressmen felt they had no choice but to sign the resolution. We don't know if any of them had private misgivings.

■ Page 21, Analysing the value and limitations of a source with reference to its origin, purpose and content

9 The origin is valuable for historians because it comes from a book written by Daisy Bates in 1962, five years after the Little Rock desegregation crisis. Bates was closely involved with what took place at Central High. A limitation of the origin of the source is that Bates was too closely involved. She was the president of the Arkansas NAACP and her book might be too biased. The purpose of her book was to bring attention to the events at Central High and the role played by the governor. This is of value because Bates was an eyewitness to the events.

A limitation could be that Bates wanted to exaggerate the governor's role in order to present a dark conspiracy. The value of the content is that historians would have gained important information from Bates about the events at Central High. A limitation is that Bates only discusses the events from her point of view. We do not have other perspectives such as from the governor or other participants.

■ 2 Protests and action

■ Page 29, Reading for comprehension

1   African American bus riders would find several aspects of the city code objectionable. Bus seating that was separated by race meant some would feel they were inferior. According to the city code, a bus operator could also decide if there should be whole buses allocated to separate races. Finally, by making it unlawful to refuse to sit where they were assigned, African Americans were made to feel discriminated against.

■ Page 31, Comparing and contrasting sources

2   In Sources B and C, the Montgomery Bus Boycott's importance is analysed. The two sources suggest that black people had the capacity for unified action. Source B mentions the 'unity across class lines', while Source C states that black people had the 'capacity for sustained collective action'. The two sources also agree that the protesters' actions were prompted by terrible treatment. Source B states that the people had the right to protest for what was right. Source C similarly mentions that people were demonstrating against the 'humiliation of Jim Crow'. The two sources also share the idea that black people must be the ones to take charge against immoral laws. Source B claims that black people 'must act as their own agents of change'. This is similar in Source C which states that tens of thousands of people worked together without outside help. Finally, both sources stress the local nature of the protests. Source B discusses the role of local women. Source C focuses on the local leadership that helped organize the boycott.

There are also some significant differences in the two sources. Source B suggests that local women were the driving force behind the boycott. Source C, on the other hand, ignores the role of women and, instead discusses the importance of the Montgomery Improvement Association and its leadership. Additionally, Source C is different from Source B in discussing the power of the Montgomery black people. Source C discusses the economic power the black people had in carrying out the boycott. Source B does not mention the economic factor. Instead, the source mentions that black people could not vote so they had no political power. However, they were able to make changes through protests.

■ Page 33, Analysing memoirs and eyewitness accounts

3   Memoirs are not always reliable sources of information for historians. In the case of Sources D and E, the author was an active participant in the events he described. It is possible that he might have had motives beyond just describing what took place during the sit-ins. Because of his involvement, he might have chosen to exaggerate the events or his own role. Another limitation might be that Proudfoot wrote his book shortly after the sit-ins. There is no hindsight here and the historian might question how close in time Proudfoot was and how this might impact its reliability.

4   Sources D and E offer insights into the organization of sit-ins. Source D is valuable because it details the plans on how to conduct sit-ins and how non-violence was stressed. In Source E, Proudfoot provides historians with a first-hand account of what it was like to participate in a sit-in and what might happen. Historians would gain a sense of the dangers involved and who the perpetrators of violence against peaceful protesters were.

■ Page 35, Analysing a historian's arguments

5   The Sovereignty Commission was deeply involved in trying to uncover any criminal activity that could be tied to Freedom Riders. The Commission compiled files on every Freedom Rider. It also worked closely with the highway patrol and the White Citizens' Councils to counter the Freedom Rides.

6   The Sovereignty Commission was convinced that the Freedom Riders and the Civil Rights Movement were part of a grand communist scheme to destroy southern traditions and culture. It believed, and tried to prove, that the Freedom Riders were dangerous agitators from outside the South who were against American values.

- Page 37, Lack of hindsight

7 The Albany marches proved to be a failure, according to Cleghorn. The local authorities were able to jail all the marchers by using nearby jails once the Albany one was full. After successfully forcing the mass marches to be cancelled, the local police chief gave a seminar to many southern policemen on how to confront racial protests.

8 A historian could use Cleghorn's account as a helpful eyewitness account to describe the Albany marches. However, a historian would also investigate and analyse the Albany events using other sources. The historian would want to know in the long term how successful the Albany Movement was. This could be done by finding out whether voter registration increased in the years following the marches. The historian would also compare what happened in Albany to other, later, marches. By doing so, the historian might be able to draw more conclusions about the effectiveness of the Albany Movement. Finally, the historian could seek information from the accounts made by the leaders of the movement to determine their sense of what took place in Albany and how effective the marches were.

9 The photograph provides proof that Dr. King and Dr. Anderson met Police Chief Pritchett on at least one occasion. The civil rights leaders appear determined as Pritchett blocks their path. It also is clear that the engagement was captured on film – someone is recording the event in the background. Further investigation would reveal that moments later, King and Anderson were arrested.

- Page 39, Spot the inference

Statement	I	P	S	X
President Johnson ordered the FBI to arrest the murderers				✗
Moses thought public opinion could be changed by parents' action		✗		
Without government intervention, violence would continue	✗			
The government was slow to act in the Philadelphia, Mississippi case and delayed action for a day			✗	

- Page 41, Relevance of origin and purpose in determining a historian's views

10 Source J's origin is a biography of President Johnson and its purpose is to examine his presidency. Civil rights would certainly factor into the analysis, although the author would also be investigating other issues in the Johnson presidency. These could include foreign affairs and his Great Society programmes. The origin and purpose might, therefore, suggest a look at Johnson's policies in a broad analysis. Source K, on the other hand, focuses on the civil rights policies of three presidents. Because the source comes from a journal article, it would not have the same depth of analysis, perhaps, as a book-length treatment of the same subject. The author teaches at a southern university and published the article in the *Journal of Southern History*. These factors may suggest that he has an expertise in the subject.

11 Source J covers the Johnson presidency, from 1963 to 1969. The book was published in 2004. The author, Robert Dallek, is a US historian who specializes in American presidents. It would seem he is well qualified to discuss President Johnson. Source K covers a greater span of history, from 1944 to 1969. It is a more recent work than Source J as it was published in 2014. The author, David Goldfield, is also a US historian.

- Page 45, Using a source and your own knowledge

12 The text and the source offer insights about what took place in Selma. The text provides an overview of the events, while the source gives the reader a first hand account. The source provides evidence in support of the analysis in the text.

13 In the text, it is clear that King and other leaders hoped for a showdown in Selma. Part of their strategy was to focus national attention on the dreadful state of voter registration there. This could be accomplished by thousands getting arrested. In the source, John Lewis uses King's words to explain the strategy. He wanted to first get national attention by marching and then, possibly, going to jail. The next step, he hoped, would be for the US government to finally take action by forcing the local authorities to register blacks. Together, the text and source provide a fuller account of the Selma strategy than either one would have done alone.

14 The couple might be illiterate. Also, the registration forms were often very complex and designed to stop people from registering. The volunteers were trained to complete the form.

Page 49, Synthesizing information

15 By registering to vote, African Americans felt the freedom to resist their oppressors. No longer would they be forced into submission and have their basic humanity questioned. By registering to vote, they hoped they could improve their economic and social situation.

16 Among the results of the Voting Rights Act were: the large increase in voter registration, more black people were elected to political office, literacy and other tests were made illegal, and all citizens 21 years of age and older could now vote. Some of these are supported by Source O. The source clearly states that many more people were able to vote as a result of the passage of the Voting Rights Act. The source also discusses the end of the use of registration tests that kept people from voting. Finally, Source O states that by having the right to vote, political participation would grow. This resulted in a significant increase in the number of black politicians in the South.

3 The role and significance of key actors/groups

Page 55, Examining a source's purpose

1 The letter was a public statement, published first by the American Friends Service Committee.

2 King hoped that by publishing the letter, the contents would receive the maximum publicity.

3 The white ministers were upset that King and others were willing to break laws. King replied that unjust and immoral laws can and should be broken. He further questioned the legitimacy of those laws since they were passed by an all-white legislature. Blacks were not able to vote for the legislature that made the laws so the laws should be considered invalid.

Page 57, Analysing a source

4 Martin Luther King, Jr and Malcolm X saw themselves in very different ways. King viewed himself first and foremost as an American. What he wanted was to have the same rights as other Americans. He did not believe that race should be factor in how he was treated. Malcolm X believed he was an American by accident. He firmly believed that his African and black heritage were more important than whether or not he was a US citizen. He had no desire to integrate with the larger white society, preferring his people's own cultural and social institutions.

Page 59, Summarizing a source

5 The black leaders were surprised that Johnson did not say he would be forced to compromise on the civil rights bill. Instead, he said he wanted it just as it was. He also said he wanted the leaders to join him in fighting poverty. They had not expected such an invitation.

6 Johnson wanted to widen the scope of his civil rights agenda so that it would not be solely tied to racial minorities. He felt he could get his legislation passed if it included all poor people. Johnson cleverly got the support of the black leaders so he now had important allies in the upcoming legislative fights.

Page 61, Integrating knowledge and sources

7 The NAACP and Martin Luther King, Jr argued about the best strategies to move the civil rights struggle forward. The NAACP preferred its slower and steadier legal strategy. It hoped to bring up court cases that would result in legal decisions in favour of dismantling Jim Crow laws. King, on the other hand, was in favour of direct action and mass mobilization. This was particularly true after the successful outcome of the Montgomery Bus Boycott. When the 47th NAACP convention met in 1956, many of the younger NAACP members were moved by what had happened at Montgomery. They tried to pass numerous resolutions calling for support of mass action. However, leaders of the NAACP, such as Roger Wilkins and Thurgood Marshall, did all they could to maintain control. They wanted to continue on the same path that had resulted in the *Brown* decision. At the convention, King tried to maintain a low profile so as not to antagonize the NAACP leadership. In the end, a weak resolution was passed that stated that the NAACP executive board would give 'careful consideration' to using the mass tactics followed in Montgomery. This really meant that King would continue with his strategy and the NAACP with theirs.

■ Page 63, Making inferences

8 According to the source, the civil rights issue hurts the whole USA and not just the South. This is because without solving the deep civil rights problems, the USA can never reach its fullest potential. It will remain undemocratic and its economy and political systems will continue to be stunted. The group states that a small number of congressmen have taken control of the legislature and won't permit changes to be made that would help the entire nation.

■ Page 65, Comparing and contrasting sources

9 Sources E and F share some similarities in terms of why each group was formed. In the case of Source E, the Southern Negro Leaders Conference on Transportation and Non-Violent Integration, which later became the SCLC, believed that it had no moral choice but to confront racism in America. The SNCC in Source F also appealed to one's conscience and moral nature. Both sources conveyed the sense of urgency. Source E is more explicit is demanding action immediately, while Source F makes an implicit call to protest and action. Finally, both Sources E and F agree that faith is an important element in the struggle against justice. Source E mentions that they have a 'God-given duty to save us all' while Source F stresses that faith will help those who doubt.

The two sources differ on a number of points. Source F emphasizes that SNCC is a non-violent organization but Source E focuses on how racism is keeping the country backwards. Source F suggests that action needs to be taken quickly in order to save the country. The means are not discussed. Source E views the struggle as one which impacts the whole nation. It is implicit that the struggle will also be nationwide. Source F, on the other hand, recognizes the importance of keeping activities focused on the local level when it mentions that 'each local group in this movement must diligently work out the clear meaning of this statement'. Finally, Source F stresses how good and moral actions can always counter negative deeds. Source E, on the other hand, describes how Congress is unable to act so it is left to people to take action or the country will remain doomed. Actions, not fine words, are what is needed.

■ Page 67, Identifying relevant content from an illustration

10 White people are portrayed as being organized and united even if they are of different religions and political parties. The black people, on the other hand, run away from Elijah Muhammad and his economic plan. Because of fear or pride they won't sit down with the leader of the Nation of Islam.

11 Black unity is non-existent. Black leaders run away from Elijah Muhammad, rather than discuss his economic plan. The idea of either Muhammad or his solution to the economic difficulties is enough to make them flee. It would appear that they have no interest in pursuing unity, or at least the sort that Elijah Muhammad is proposing.

■ Case study 2: Apartheid South Africa 1948–64

■ 4 Nature and characteristics of discrimination

■ Page 73, Examining the content of a source

1 According to Smuts, natives and white people are different from one another on several levels. Because of these differences, it does not make sense to have the same political system for both. By keeping the two groups together, both suffer. It would be far better to let the native develop at his own pace.

2 Smuts provides insight into the political arguments in South Africa in 1917. His views are a clear indication of why some South African whites wished to create physical and political barriers between the races.

3 A limitation of the content is that opposing views are not presented. It is unclear whether or not other South African politicians were in agreement with Smuts. Furthermore, the reader does not know if South African black people agree with his assertion that their community 'will be satisfied' if they are separated from white people.

■ Page 73, Contrasting two sources

4 Possible differences could include the following: Source A suggests that if natives chose to work in white areas, they would be free to do so. Source B paints a very different picture. Black labour had little freedom of movement. Source A states that separating the races would benefit both while Source B argues that separation harmed the African and assisted the white person. Source A does not explain how separation would impact many aspects of African life, such as where one could live and travel and whether or not one could purchase land, while Source B focuses on these issues.

■ Page 75, Examining a source for its purpose

5 The *New York Times* produced the source.

6 The article was produced to inform the public of possible changes in South Africa's race relations.

7 The purpose is valuable because it demonstrates that the international press was closely following the events in South Africa after the 1948 elections. Consequently, *New York Times'* readers would have some knowledge about the possible plans of the new government in South Africa.

■ Page 77, Examining the content of a source

8 Residential areas should be divided according to race. Therefore, there should be distinct European, African or Native, coloured, and Indian areas.

9 The National Party thought that separation of the races was in the best interests of all groups. Each group would therefore be able to develop at its own pace, according to its own needs and culture.

10 In 1948, the situation between Europeans and non-Europeans was dire. Races were mixing socially and on public transport. Non-Europeans were trying to become more like Europeans, which was not in the best interests of their people.

■ Page 79, Identifying the main points in a source

11 The Sophiatown removals were well organized. This is clearly shown by the line of trucks. The residents' meagre belongings were loaded onto the trucks. The removals were carried out under the watch of police officers.

■ Page 79, Examining origin of a source

12 Trevor Huddleston, a parish priest, was the author of the source.

13 He wrote this in 1956.

14 This source is valuable because it provides the reader with a first hand account of the Sophiatown removals. It was written three years after the events so it might accurately reflect what took place. Furthermore, Huddleston had served the people of Sophiatown so he knew the background of the removals, as well the impact on the residents.

15 By being so close to the people of Sophiatown, Huddleston may have presented a one-sided perspective. He also wrote the book shortly after the events so there is little hindsight or distance from the events.

■ Page 81, Making inferences

16 Coloureds, Asians or Indians, and white people were not mentioned in the Act.

17 Any and all provincial authorities would lose what control they had concerning native education.

18 The Ministry of Education would be the final authority in African education.

■ Page 81, Reading for content

19 Mandela thought the ultimate goal of the government's education policy was to force Africans into a permanent state of servitude.

20 According to the evidence Mandela presented, the government was following a step-by-step process to change African education at every stage. First, primary schools were forced to introduce Bantu education. This was to be followed by secondary and high schools. Finally, the universities were to be segregated if the new bill passed Parliament.

■ Page 83, Comparing two sources

Three similarities: (1) Both sources claim that the Bantustan system was being promoted as being beneficial for Africans and whites. In Source I, de Kock writes that the policy was for the 'development' of Africans. Source J suggests that the policy was believed to be a way to protect Africans.

(2) By creating separate homelands or Bantustans, greater protections would exist for those living there. Source I supports this by stating that the particular cultural values would be protected without interference or competition by whites. Source J also states that different cultures were 'unique systems' and could be best protected if they were separated from other cultures.

(3) Both sources mention that on tribal homelands the people would be governed by their own leaders. Source I identifies these leaders as 'traditional authorities', while Source J describes them as 'tribal authorities'.

■ 5 Protests and action

■ Page 89, Examining content of a source

1 The large number of leaders being charged by the government, as well as the 2000 supporters, suggest that the campaign was large. Furthermore, the fact that mass arrests were taking place in different locations would support this idea.

2 The value of the content is that it demonstrates that the government hoped to try the leaders of the campaign as communist sympathizers instead of people trying to force the government to overturn apartheid laws. It also is clear that the movement has many followers and many people willing to face arrest for breaking apartheid laws.

3 A limitation of the content is that we do not know the circumstances in which the twenty leaders were arrested, nor do we know the outcome of the hearing. We also do not have a sense as to the scope of the campaign and whether or not it is widespread or only taking place in a small number of locations.

■ Page 91, Interpreting a photographic source

4 Source B suggests that there were many people charged with treason. They included white, black, Asian and coloured people. They do not appear to be distressed but are, in fact, smiling, suggesting that they are united and looking forward to their day in court. It also is evident that there are both male and female people who are to face trial.

■ Page 93, Summarize the arguments

5 Source C explains how the Nationalist government greatly fears Africans and how it has tried to keep them in their place. The government measures include threats, punishment, force, and banning, among many others. The boycott demonstrated to whites that Africans do not accept their denial of rights. It also showed Africans that if they can unite, they may be successful in gaining their basic rights.

■ Page 95, Comparing and contrasting two sources

6 Similarities:

(1) Both sources state that the police used weapons.

(2) There was a tragic loss of life at Sharpeville.

(3) There had been a demonstration in front of the police station.

Differences:

(1) Source D states that the police had been fired upon first. Source E states that the police fired first.

(2) Source D claims the demonstrators were armed. Source E says he could not find any weapons among the demonstrators.

(3) Source D states that there were 20,000 protesters. Source E uses the figure of 3000.

(4) Source E mentions that there were many children and women while Source D does not mention this.

(5) Source D claims that the policemen's lives were in great danger while Source E disputes this idea.

■ Page 97, Combining information from a source and outside knowledge

7 In the face of growing instability after the Sharpeville killings, the government passed a new law described in Source F. The law allowed the government to declare the Pan Africanist Congress and the African National Congress illegal if they were viewed as being a threat to public order. Both groups had organized demonstrations protesting about the many Africans who had been killed at Sharpeville and Langa. Many workers stayed at home instead of working to show their anger. The government arrested 2000 political leaders in its efforts to put an end once and for all to opposition to apartheid. It was able to legitimize its actions by passing and then applying the Unlawful Organizations Act, thereby giving it a legal cover.

■ Page 99, Examining a source's purpose

8 Because Mandela's speech was made at his 1963 trial, historians were given insights into the formation of *Umkhonto we Sizwe* and Mandela's role in its creation. The purpose of the speech was to explain to the court why he felt violence was the only option left to the Africans. At the same time, its value may be limited because Mandela was offering a public statement that might not necessarily have reflected his private views. Mandela knew he was speaking to an audience and that his words would be reported in the press.

■ Page 101, Comparing and contrasting two sources

9 Both sources explain that the Rivonia Trial resulted in the anti-apartheid leadership being crippled. Source H states that 'the most effective and prominent leaders' had been jailed for the remainder of their lives. This is supported by Source I, which states that there was a 'vacuum of leadership' once these leaders had been imprisoned. The two sources also suggest that apartheid was strengthened by the court's verdict. H explains that there would be 'no serious unrest' in the country for the next twelve years while Source I states that 'white strength was to be consolidated'.

10 The two sources differ on a number of points. Source H claims that some in the South African press had planted 'seeds of concern' about the court's decision. Source I states that 'the press praised the police, the prosecutor, and the judge'. The two sources are also at odds in reference to the international dimension of the court's decision. While Source H acknowledges that many people outside South Africa saw the country's judicial system as being impartial, it was also clear that the courts, in the end, supported apartheid. Source I, on the other hand, downplays the idea that the USA and other western countries would put any pressure on South Africa to moderate its racial policies.

■ 6 The role and significance of key actors/groups

■ Page 107, Identifying the main points in a source

1 Members of the ANC were forced to become violent because the government refused to grant Africans their freedom. These ANC activists had to seek justice with weapons because there was no alternative. They had to create a strong force to make possible a peaceful South Africa.

2 Western civilization did not develop by itself. It received contributions from many sources. The same should apply to the Africans. The government does not want Africans to have the freedom to choose how they develop since it is the government itself which is directing African development through the Native Affairs Bureau. Africans have never been consulted about their development.

Page 109, Determining the value and limitation of a source's content

3 Mandela took the advice of the National Action Council and decided not to turn himself in to the authorities. He felt he could much better serve the cause if he remained free to organize opposition to the government.

4 Mandela sacrificed his livelihood and family life for his cause. He compared this to the suffering of many other anti-apartheid activists.

5 The source provides insight into Mandela's motivations when he decided not to surrender to the authorities. The content also demonstrates Mandela's overall strategy. He wanted to encourage others to remain steadfast and not surrender their rights to a government he viewed as illegal. The source is also important because it discusses Mandela's relationship with the National Action Council and how it offered him advice.

6 It would seem that Mandela was in high spirits when the photo was taken. He is not being confined and is free to walk outside the courthouse. In the crowd behind him is a mix of people of different races. They may be Mandela's fellow defendants or lawyers defending their clients.

Page 111, Examining the origin of a source

7 Robert Sobukwe is the author of Source D.

8 Sobukwe provides valuable insight for a historian studying the significance of the PAC because he was the founder of the group and understood why and how the PAC differed from the ANC. Another value is that the source represents the very creation of the group.

9 While the historian might have an understanding of the beginning of the PAC, the source can be limiting because it is unclear what occurred after Sobukwe's speech. The historian does not know how the speech was received or even how many people were at the first meeting of the PAC.

Page 113, Summarizing a source

10 The ANC has continuously been at the forefront of fighting against apartheid by promoting the Freedom Charter and rejecting insulting offers from the government.

11 Because of the desperate state in which some Africans find themselves, they are willing to accept any small offer from the government.

12 Mandela is calling on the Nationalists to prove they are not afraid of free elections and public opinion.

Page 115, Examining the purpose of a source

13 Mandela wanted to honour Joe Slovo publicly and recognize the many contributions he had made to the ANC. Mandela also wanted to emphasize the close historical ties between the ANC and the SACP.

14 Because Mandela's speech was made in 1994, it might be of limited value to a historian. Many years had passed since the height of the anti-apartheid struggle in South Africa and so the true reality of the ANC–SACP relationship might have been ignored. Mandela was also honouring Slovo in a public setting. This, too, could affect the source's reliability. Furthermore, evidence of tensions between the ANC and the SACP might have been papered over in order to present a united front to a friendly audience.

Exam practice answers

█ 1 Nature and characteristics of discrimination, page 27

13 a Reasons why the presence of paratroopers was important could include:

- for protection in the face of violence
- no one else was by the students' side
- demonstrated the government's intention to uphold the law.

Award 1 mark for each relevant point up to 3 marks.

13 b The cartoon could suggest:

- desegregation had to be forcibly carried out by soldiers
- black and white people did not come together naturally
- the court's decreed segregation had to take place
- gradualism was not an option.

Award 1 mark for each relevant point up to 2 marks.

14 Possible source analyses include:

- <u>Origin</u>: source is from a 1985 interview with Melba Pattillo Beals. <u>Value</u>: the interview is a first-hand/eyewitness account by one of the Little Rock Nine. Enough time had passed since 1957 for Beals to be more analytical in thinking. <u>Limitations</u>: Because the events she discussed took place in 1957, she may have forgotten some of the details. The interview could also have been one-sided.
- <u>Purpose</u>: the interview was given in order to inform people about Little Rock from the perspective of a participant in the events there. <u>Value</u>: because Beals was one of the Little Rock Nine, she could present the hardships students faced. <u>Limitation</u>: it is possible that Beals wanted to provide an inaccurate account which would mislead the listener into believing conditions at the school were horrible.
- <u>Content</u>: Beals described her experiences at Central High. <u>Value</u>: because Beals was at Central High, a historian might gain insight into the true feelings of one of the Little Rock Nine. Beals provides details about her emotions on the first day of school. <u>Limitations</u>: the analysis Beals presents might be tainted and unreliable because what happened to her was very emotional.

For a maximum of 4 marks, candidates should refer to origin, purpose and content in their analysis of value and limitations.

15 Possible relevant comparison/contrast responses could include:

For compare:

- Both sources describe the mobs outside the school.
- The two sources discuss the attempts of the black students to enter the school.
- Both describe the angry adults against desegregation.
- Both mention students entering from a side door so they would not have to confront the mob in front of the school.

For contrast:

- Source M focuses on the students, while Source P pays more attention to the angry mob.
- Source M describes how some white students left the school because of the presence of the black students. Source P makes no mention of this.
- In Source P, it is clear that the mob had organizational help from 'men in straw hats'. Source M views the crowd as disorganized and the situation chaotic. There is no evidence of any orders coming from anyone.

Do not demand all of the above. If only one source is discussed, award a maximum of 2 marks. If the two sources are discussed separately, award 3 marks or 4–5 marks with excellent linkage. For a maximum of 6 marks, expected a detailed running comparison/contrast.

16 Possible relevant material could include:

- Source M: some white people were hysterical about black students going to the same school as their children. Some white students left school instead of attending classes with black students.
- Source N: racial divisions were so deep that only a court order and soldiers could force black and white students to be together.
- Source O: white parents attacked students. Troops were necessary to protect the Little Rock Nine.
- Source P: black reporters were attacked by the crowd because of their race. A mob was trying to stop desegregation.

Own knowledge could include evidence from:

- Jim Crow segregation laws
- *Brown I* and *Brown II* decisions and the white response
- the Southern Manifesto
- White Citizens' Councils
- urban ghettos in northern cities
- income inequalities based on race throughout the USA.

Do not expect all of the above and accept other relevant material. Response should be focused on the questions. Clear references should be made to the sources, and these references should be used effectively as evidence to support the analysis. The response should demonstrate accurate and relevant own knowledge. There should be effective synthesis of own knowledge and source material.

■ 2 Protest and action, page 53

13 a Failures of the Johnson government could include:

- violence was increasing
- passing laws to force people to like one another
- calling out troops and federal programmes instead of getting things done at the local level first.

Award 1 mark for each relevant point up to 3 marks.

13 b The source suggests that:

- Many men, mostly white, gathered to celebrate Johnson signing the Civil Rights Act.
- Several African American leaders were there to watch, including Martin Luther King, Jr.
- Witnesses appear in good spirits.
- Johnson had many pens on his desk to give out after the historic ceremony.

Award 1 mark for each relevant point up to 2 marks.

14 Possible source analyses include

- Origin: excerpt from 2006 history of Johnson's civil rights legislation. Value: focus on Johnson and King and how they helped bring forward new laws. Hindsight. Limitations: the history is so focused on one particular period it might miss the larger historical context.
- Purpose: work written to inform the general public about the civil rights legislation. Value: gives the reader a good sense of the important laws that had a great impact on US history. Limitations: focused perhaps exclusively on two men. Other forces at work here might have been given less attention.
- Content: Johnson taking his ideas to the South. Value: proved a sense of Johnson's leadership qualities and what motivated him. Limitations: Because the content refers to two public speeches the president gave, we don't know how he felt in private. This is not included in the excerpt.

For a maximum of 4 marks, candidates should refer to origin, purpose and content in their analysis of value and limitations.

15 Possible relevant comparison/contrast responses could include:

For compare:

- historically, old hatreds and hostilities
- new positive vision of the South
- the South was changing

- battles between neighbours
- southerners were waiting for someone to push them to change in regards to racial relations.

For contrast:

- Source M discusses stable leadership in the South. Source O views southern leadership changing with the times.
- Source M sees problems in the South, while Source O is centred on the South.
- Source M details close relationships among leaders in the South while division exists among leaders in the North.

Do not demand all of the above. If only one source is discussed, award a maximum of 2 marks. If the two sources are discussed separately, award 3 marks or 4–5 marks with excellent linkage. For a maximum of 6 marks, expected a detailed running comparison/contrast.

16 Possible relevant material could include:

- Source M: many white southerners were just waiting for change; white and black political leaders had ties over generations.
- Source N: many politicians attended the ceremony of the signing of the Civil Rights Act. Bipartisan observers, as well as important black leaders in attendance.
- Source O: Johnson pushed for legislation to change 'barriers of intolerance'.
- Source P: Republican–Democratic rivalry during presidential campaign heated up the rhetoric.

Own knowledge could include evidence from:

- President Kennedy's plans.
- Opposition for southern Democrats in Congress.
- Johnson winning Republican support for civil rights legislation.
- Johnson's vision of a Great Society.
- Push by civil rights leaders for change.
- Compromise between civil rights groups and Johnson about voting.
- How the 1964 presidential election impacted civil rights legislation.

Do not expect all of the above and accept other relevant material. Response should be focused on the questions. Clear references should be made to the sources, and these references should be used effectively as evidence to support the analysis. The response should demonstrate accurate and relevant own knowledge. There should be effective synthesis of own knowledge and source material.

■ 3 The role and significance of key actors/groups, page 71

13 a What the Justice Department was asking Judge Elliott to do could include:

- halt prosecution of SNCC representatives
- stop officers from committing violence
- issue a restraining order so police could not intimidate black voters.

Award 1 mark for each relevant point up to 3 marks.

13 b Source O suggests:

- peaceful SNCC demonstrators were being harassed by the police
- white policemen were armed with clubs
- SNCC activists were trying to get people to register to vote.

Award 1 mark for each relevant point up to 2 marks.

14 Possible relevant source analyses include:

- Origin: newspaper article in the *Atlanta Daily World*. Value: because it was from a southern African American newspaper, it provided news to that community. Limitations: the newspaper's audience was one particular group.
- Purpose: to inform its readers of recent events. Value: to inform the African American public about the activities of the Justice Department and the local response. Limitations: might be a biased account due to the newspaper's readership.
- Content: how a local judge responded to the Justice Department's appeal. Value: the source explains in detail the government request and the problems facing those who wanted to vote. Limitations: it is unclear why Judge Elliott turned down the government request.

For a maximum of 4 marks, candidates should refer to origin, purpose and content in their analysis of value and limitations.

15 Possible relevant comparison/contrast responses could include:

For compare:

- Young activists made up the membership of SNCC. The organization was student based.
- It was an energetic and action-oriented organization.
- It was locally based.

For contrasts:

- Source M focuses on voter registration while Source N mentions the Freedom Rides.
- Source N states that SNCC was independent of other civil rights groups. Source M does not mention the relationship SNCC had with other groups.
- Source N discusses the non-violent character of SNCC, while in Source M this is only implicit.

Do not demand all of the above. If only one source is discussed, award a maximum of 2 marks. If the two sources are discussed separately, award 3 marks or 4–5 marks with excellent linkage. For a maximum of 6 marks, expected a detailed running comparison/contrast.

16 Possible relevant material could include:

- Source M: SNCC was involved in voter registration and educating people in Albany, Georgia.
- Source N: SNCC was a student-led, independent civil rights organization; it had a nationwide impact.
- Source O: SNCC was active in voter registration drives and faced aggressive southern authorities.
- Source P: SNCC members went to jail for their beliefs; they tried to register voters in Georgia.

Own knowledge could include evidence from:

- Ella Baker's role in helping the group to form.
- SNCC's participation in the Freedom Rides.
- SNCC's role in the Albany Movement.
- Bloody Sunday in Selma, Alabama.
- Freedom Summer in Mississippi.
- SNCC's involvement in the Mississippi Freedom Democratic Party.

Do not expect all of the above and accept other relevant material. Response should be focused on the questions. Clear references should be made to the sources, and these references should be used effectively as evidence to support the analysis. The response should demonstrate accurate and relevant own knowledge. There should be effective synthesis of own knowledge and source material.

■ 4 Nature and characteristics of discrimination, page 87

13 a Reasons the Bantu Education Act was needed could include:

- Bantu needed to be able to express themselves culturally.
- So that Bantu and European communal life would not be disrupted.
- Education tailored to Bantu needs.
- The Bantu could reach full development in their own community.

Award 1 mark for each relevant point up to 3 marks.

13 b The photo could suggest:

- students were unhappy with the Bantu Education Act
- protests were made by students
- people knew that the Bantu Education Act was forced on them by the *baas* (boss) or apartheid regime
- the protests appeared to be peaceful.

Award 1 mark for each relevant point up to 2 marks.

14 Possible relevant source analyses include:

- <u>Origin</u>: Albert Luthuli's autobiography *Let My People Go*, published in 1962. <u>Value</u>: the book was written in 1962, during the height of the apartheid regime. The author was one of the major leaders of the ANC so he had deep knowledge of the problems facing Africans. <u>Limitations</u>: Luthuli was very close to the events so his account might be very biased. There is little hindsight because the events he describes occurred not much earlier than when the book was published.
- <u>Purpose</u>: Luthuli wrote this book to publicize the plight of the Africans. <u>Value</u>: he hoped to bring worldwide attention to a people held captive. The book provides a valuable insight into the thinking of a key member of the ANC. <u>Limitations</u>: the purpose of writing this book was one-dimensional and did not take into account the perspectives of the government. It also only provides a brief look at the situation in South Africa because the apartheid system continued for many years afterwards.
- <u>Content</u>: the extract discusses the difficult situation parents faced as a result of the Bantu Education Act. <u>Value</u>: Luthuli explains how the parents were impacted by the Act and the difficult choices they faced. <u>Limitations</u>: the extract is not a comprehensive examination of the impact of the Act but only a limited look at the problem. The language used is also emotionally charged and may be very biased as a result.

For a maximum of 4 marks, candidates should refer to origin, purpose and content in their analysis of value and limitations.

15 Possible relevant comparison/contrast responses could include:

For compare:

- Both sources suggest that the Bantu Education Act would put control of education into the hands of the state.
- Schools would be designed with the needs of the Africans in mind.
- The Act would be helpful to Africans on the reserves, many of whom had not previously had access to formal education.

For contrast:

- Source M suggests that the Bantu Education Act would put Africans while Source P claims the Act would subjugate Africans.
- Source M states that the current educational system is not useful because Africans cannot be assimilated in the white community. Source P claims that Bantu education was meant to 'suffocate independent thought'.
- Source M suggests that educated black people were frustrated by the lack of employment possibilities. Source P disputes this idea, stating that Africans became members of the black elite, including political leaders.

Do not demand all of the above. If only one source is discussed, award a maximum of 2 marks. If the two sources are discussed separately, award 3 marks or 4–5 marks with excellent linkage. For a maximum of 6 marks, expected a detailed running comparison/contrast.

16 Possible relevant material could include:

- Source M: the government had created the Bantu Education Act. It had taken over control of education. It claimed it was promoting Bantu education as a means to help Africans develop according to their needs.
- Source N: the government's plans were met with protests by students. They did not want to be part of *baas*, or apartheid, education.
- Source O: Chief Luthuli acknowledged the degree to which the government had taken hold of the educational system and how many parents felt they had no choice but to send their children to the Bantu schools.
- Source P: Verwoerd wanted to impose government control over education in order to ensure that the curriculum would not encourage Africans to have high ambitions but, rather, to become little more than 'docile animals'.

Own knowledge could include evidence from:

- Eiselen Commission and its recommendations.
- Government subsidies to mission schools prior to the Bantu Education Act.
- Boycotts of Bantu Schools.

- The Extension of Universities Act 1959.
- Disparity in amounts the government spent on white versus native schools.
- The condition of education prior to 1953.
- The increase in the number of schools and students as a result of the Bantu Education Act.

Do not expect all of the above and accept other relevant material. Response should be focused on the questions. Clear references should be made to the sources, and these references should be used effectively as evidence to support the analysis. The response should demonstrate accurate and relevant own knowledge. There should be effective synthesis of own knowledge and source material.

■ 5 Protests and action, page 105

13 a Short-term effects of Sharpeville could include:

- money left the country
- stock market and gold prices fell
- state of emergency was declared
- ANC and PAC were banned.

Award 1 mark for each relevant point up to 3 marks.

13 b The photo could suggest:

- many graves
- line of trucks with coffins
- crowds gathered
- priests and officials at each grave site.

Award 1 mark for each relevant point up to 2 marks.

14 Possible relevant source analyses include:

- <u>Origin</u>: UN Resolution 134, 1 April 1960. <u>Value</u>: official statement by the UN Security Council. France and Britain abstained. <u>Limitations</u>: one-sided statement. Because it was issued shortly after Sharpeville, there is no hindsight.
- <u>Purpose</u>: notify the world community of the Security Council's stance. <u>Value</u>: clear demonstration of the Security Council's condemnation of the massacre. <u>Limitations</u>: no sense of whether or not the issue was debated.
- <u>Content</u>: text of UN Resolution 134. <u>Value</u>: clearly states how much of the international community condemned South Africa's actions and apartheid policy. The Security Council quickly reacted to a complaint made by 29 member states. <u>Limitations</u>: unclear why France and Britain abstained. Little analysis of what led to Sharpeville.

For a maximum of 4 marks, candidates should refer to origin, purpose and content in their analysis of value and limitations.

15 Possible relevant comparison/contrast responses could include:

For compare:

- immediate effects
- international repercussions
- ANC and PAC targeted by the government.

For contrast:

- Source M discusses long-term impact of Sharpeville. Source P focuses on immediate impact.
- Source P analyses the economic and political impact of Sharpeville while Source M discusses the social and political impact.
- Source P mentions the panic in South Africa. Source M discusses the increased intolerance by the apartheid regime.

Do not demand all of the above. If only one source is discussed, award a maximum of 2 marks. If the two sources are discussed separately, award 3 marks or 4–5 marks with excellent linkage. For a maximum of 6 marks, expected a detailed running comparison/contrast.

16 Possible relevant material could include:

- Source M: impossible for the international community to ignore; practical ties continued.
- Source N: photo of funeral impacted world opinion; evident that the scale of the tragedy was huge.

- Source O: UN Security Council moved to issue a nine to none denunciation. South Africa held to account.
- Source P: fear of international isolation in South Africa.

Own knowledge could include evidence from:

- ANC/PAC driven underground. Armed groups *Umkhonto we Sizwe* and *Poqo* received support from anti-colonial groups/countries in Africa.
- Calls for boycotts of South African goods. Mandela and Martin Luther King, Jr joint statement.
- South Africa withdrew from the British Commonwealth.
- South African sports teams banned from competitions.
- Luthuli awarded Nobel Peace Prize.

Do not expect all of the above and accept other relevant material. Response should be focused on the questions. Clear references should be made to the sources, and these references should be used effectively as evidence to support the analysis. The response should demonstrate accurate and relevant own knowledge. There should be effective synthesis of own knowledge and source material.

■ 6 The role and significance of key actors/groups, page 117

13 a What Mandela hoped to accomplish in his testimony could include:

- opportunity to broadcast ANC's vision globally
- advance the nationalist cause
- focus attention on himself as an important ANC leader because the banned organization's supporters needed hope.

Award 1 mark for each relevant point up to 3 marks.

13 b The photo could suggest:

- thousands marching in support of their leaders
- the march was peaceful
- demonstrators disrupted traffic in Johannesburg.

Award 1 mark for each relevant point up to 2 marks.

14 The source could suggest:

- Origin: from Mandela's testimony at the Treason Trial in 1960. Extract was included in his autobiography. Value: quotes from the judge and prosecutor, as well as his answers. Limitations: extract was only a small part of his testimony to be included in his autobiography.
- Purpose: testimony from the Treason Trial. Value: extract clearly demonstrates Mandela's clever responses and his commitment to his cause. Limitations: unclear how his answers were received by the judge and the prosecutor.
- Content: a discussion on the hopes of the ANC and the introduction of violence. Value: gives a clear indication of his views on violence and his thoughts on the future of apartheid. Limitations: because it was only part of his testimony in 1960, the reader is unclear about the historical context. Analytical hindsight is missing.

For a maximum of 4 marks, candidates should refer to origin, purpose and content in their analysis of value and limitations.

15 Possible relevant comparison/contrast responses could include:

For compare:

- put ANC's fight against apartheid before a world audience
- Mandela spoke from the dock and not the witness stand
- brilliant and successful speeches
- Mandela focused attention on himself as a leader.

For contrast:

- Source O states that the anti-apartheid struggle was not manipulated by outsiders or communists. Source M stresses that it was a nationalist struggle and does not mention communist influence.

- Source O states that Mandela was willing to die for his cause, whereas Source M suggests that Mandela wanted to advance the nationalist cause.
- Source M makes reference to Mandela's statements at two trials. Source O focuses on only the Rivonia Trial, when he faced the death penalty.

Do not demand all of the above. If only one source is discussed, award a maximum of 2 marks. If the two sources are discussed separately, award 3 marks or 4–5 marks with excellent linkage. For a maximum of 6 marks, expected a detailed running comparison/contrast.

16 Possible relevant material could include:

- Source M: 'messianic' leadership; wanted to bring worldwide attention to the evils of apartheid.
- Source N: mass of supporters who rallied behind Mandela and other leaders.
- Source O: he acted as an individual and a leader.
- Source P: was a spokesman for the ANC at the Rivonia Trial.

Own knowledge could include evidence from:

- Mandela's role in helping to set up *Umkhonto we Sizwe* and move away from non-violent struggle.
- Overcoming banning order and participating in most major ANC decisions in the 1950s.
- Helping to create the ANC Youth League, thereby transforming the organization into an activist movement.
- Mandela serving as the international face of the ANC at several trials.

Do not expect all of the above and accept other relevant material. Response should be focused on the questions. Clear references should be made to the sources, and these references should be used effectively as evidence to support the analysis. The response should demonstrate accurate and relevant own knowledge. There should be effective synthesis of own knowledge and source material.

Acknowledgements

The Publishers would like to thank the following for permission to reproduce copyright material.

Photo credits: p13 Copyright by Bill Mauldin (1962). Courtesy of Bill Mauldin Estate LLC/Library of Congress LC-DIG-ppmsca-03216; **p24** Copyright by Bill Mauldin (1962). Courtesy of Bill Mauldin Estate LLC/Library of Congress LC-DIG-ppmsca-03244; **p37** Donald Uhrbrock/The LIFE Images Collection/Getty Images; **p45** Granger, NYC/TopFoto; **p52** Cecil Stoughton, White House Press Office (WHPO); **p71** Danny Lyon/Magnum Photos; **p79** Terence Spencer/The LIFE Images Collection/Getty Images; **p84** Paul Weinberg/CC BY-SA 3.0/Wikimedia Commons; **p86** Drum Social Histories/Baileys African History Archive/Africa Media Online; **p91** Sipa Press/REX/Shutterstock; **p103** Keystone/Hulton Archive/Getty Images; **pp104, 109** Jürgen Schadeberg/Getty Images; **p116** Drum Social Histories/Baileys African History Archive/Africa Media Online.

Acknowledgements: *Africa Today*, Vol. 7, No. 3, May 1960. African National Congress, www.anc.org.za/content/struggle-my-life-nelson-mandelas-press-statement. Afrikaner Broadcasting Corporation, http://hendrikverwoerd.blogspot.com/2010/12/september-3-1948-policy-of-apartheid-hf.html. Alabama Department of Archives and History, *Code of the City of Montgomery, Alabama*, Michie City Publishing Co., Charlottesville, 1952. Albert Luthuli, *Let My People Go: An Autobiography*, McGraw-Hill, New York, 1962. *Atlanta Daily World*, 'Judge Elliott Refuses U.S. Request to Restrain Terrell County Law Officer Threats', 15 August 1962. Bedford/St. Martin's, *Apartheid in South Africa: A Brief History with Documents* by David Gordon, 2017. Civil Rights Movement Veterans, www.crmvet.org/riders/6205_core_coi_bigelow.pdf; www.crmvet.org/docs/64_msfs_parents_letter.pdf; www.crmvet.org/docs/mbbleaf.htm; www.crmvet.org/docs/sncc1.htm. Bedford, David Howard-Pitney, *Martin Luther King Jr., Malcolm X, and the Civil Rights Struggle of the 1950s and 1960s*. 2004. Department of Information, Pretoria, *History of South Africa* by W.J. de Kock, 1971. Greenwood Press, *Jim Crow Laws* by Leslie Tischauser, 2012. Harry Ransom Center, University of Texas, Austin, Mike Wallace, 5 May 1957. Heinemann International, *No Easy Walk to Freedom* by Nelson Mandela, 1989. Hoover Institution Press, *From Protest to Challenge. A Documentary History of South African Politics in South Africa, 1882–1964*, Vol. 3, *Challenge and Violence, 1953–1964* by Thomas Karis and Gail M. Gerhart, 1977. Houghton Mifflin Harcourt, *Judgment Days: Lyndon Baines Johnson, Martin Luther King, Jr., and the Laws that Changed America* by Nick Kotz, 2006. Houghton Mifflin, *From the South African Past: Narratives, Documents, and Debates* by John A. Williams, 1997. HSRC Press, *Voices of Liberation: Alfred Luthuli*, second edition by Gerald Pillay, 2014. John F. Kennedy Presidential Library and Museum, http://microsites.jfklibrary.org/olemiss/controversy/doc2.html, 2010. *Journal of Southern History*, 'Border Men: Truman, Eisenhower, Johnson, and Civil Rights' by David Goldfield, February 2014. Library of America, *Reporting Civil Rights Part One: American Journalism 1941–1963* edited by Clayborne Carson, 2003. Library of America, *Reporting Civil Rights, Part One* edited by Clayborne Carson, 2013. *New York Times*, '200,000 March for Civil Rights in Orderly Washington Rally; President Sees Gain for Negro', 29 August 1963; 'South Africa Tries Race Ban Defiers', 27 August 1952; 'South African Hints Racial Registration', 17 November 1948. Oxford University Press, *Apartheid 1948–1994* by Saul Dubow, 2014; *Freedom Riders: 1961 and the Struggle for Racial Justice* by Raymond Arsenault, 2006; *Grand Expectations: The United States, 1945–1974* by James T. Patterson, 1996; *Lyndon B. Johnson: Portrait of a President* by Robert Dallek, 2004; *Nelson Mandela: A Very Short Introduction* by Ileke Boehmer, 2008; *Saving Nelson Mandela: The Rivonia Trial and the Fate of South Africa* by Kenneth Broun, 2012. Pathfinder Press, *The Struggle is My Life* by Nelson Mandela, 1990. PBS, *Eyes on the Prize: America's Civil Rights Years, 1954–1963*, first broadcast in 1987. Penguin Books, *The Autobiography of Malcolm X* by Malcolm X (with Alex Haley), 1968; *The Eyes on the Prize Civil Rights Reader*, edited by Clayborne Carson, 1991. Politicsweb, www.politicsweb.co.za/documents/hendrik-verwoerd-10-quotes. Routledge, *South Africa: The Rise and Fall of Apartheid*, third edition, by Nancy Clark and William Worger, 2016. Rowman & Littlefield, *Jim Crow's Legacy: The Lasting Impact of Segregation*, by Ruth Thompson-Miller, Joe Feagin and Leslie Picca, 2014. Royal Institute of International Affairs, *The World Today*, Vol. 9, No. 2, February 1953. Simon & Schuster, *A Matter of Justice: Eisenhower and the Beginning of the Civil Rights Revolution* by David Nichols, 2007; *Parting the Waters: America in the King Years, 1954–63* by Taylor Branch, 1988; *Walking in the Wind: A Memoir of the Movement* by John Lewis, 1998. South African Communist Party, www.sacp.org.za/main.php?ID=2671. South African History Online, www.sahistory.org.za/archive/bantu-education-act%2C-act-no-47-of-1953; www.sahistory.org.za/archive/unlawful-organizations-act%2C-act-no-34-of-1960; www.sahistory.org.za/archive/document-58-robert-mangaliso-sobukwe-opening-address-africanist-inaugural-convention-4-april. Southern Oral History Program Collection, University of North Carolina, Chapel Hill. Stanford University, Martin Luther King, Jr. Research & Education Institute, https://kinginstitute.stanford.edu/our-god-marching; http://kingencyclopedia.stanford.edu/primarydocuments/Vol4/11-Jan-1957_AStatementToTheSouth.pdf. Teachingamericanhistory.org, http://teachingamericanhistory.org/library/document/letter-from-birmingham-city-jail/. United Nations High Commissioner for Refugees, www.refworld.org/docid/3b00f1893c.html. University of Illinois Press, *Diary of a Sit-In*, second edition, by Merrill Proudfoot, 1990. University of KwaZulu-Natal Press, *Africa South: Viewpoints, 1956–1961* by M.J. Daymond and C. Sandwith, 2011. University of North Carolina Press, *Daybreak of Freedom: The Montgomery Bus Boycott* edited by Stuart Burns, 1997. US Governmental Printing Office, *Congressional Record, 84th Congress Second Session*, Vol. 102, part 4, 1956. Viking, *Malcolm X: A Life of Reinvention* by Manning Marable, 2011. Washington University Libraries, a 1985 interview with Melba Pattillo Beals, 1958. Yale University Press, *An Ordinary Atrocity: Sharpeville and its Massacre* by Philip Frankel, 2001.

Every effort has been made to trace all copyright holders, but if any have been inadvertently overlooked, the Publishers will be pleased to make the necessary arrangements at the first opportunity.